AN INTRODUCTION TO MINI-ECONOMICS

by

Dr. Anton J. Butter

AF785215

B.R. Grüner Publishing Co.
Amsterdam

The author expresses his thanks to the Faculty of Economic Sciences of the University of Amsterdam for pleasantly surprising him with participation in the economic risk of the publication of this book. He thanks Professor Jan Lambooy for his initiative in this matter.

© 1985 A.J. Butter

ISBN 90 6032 2630

All rights reserved. No part of this book may be reproduced in any form or by any electronic or mechanical means including information storage and retrieval systems without the prior permission of the publisher.

Printed in The Netherlands

CONTENTS

Without regrets and beyond looking back, to the tempting one, who beckoned me down the road to ruin I did not take. Or did I?

1

INTRODUCTION

This modest little book is the offspring of an ill-matched marriage between the high hopes I entertained some five years ago when I took up the study of very small nations as a group, and a string of adversities in private life and health, tripping me up and blocking the progress that would have been in reach if things had been different.

Facing inevitable retirement early in 1985, but with miraculously regained health and vigour, around Easter 1984 I found myself in the predicament to make a final choice: either to burn or to publish the meagre results of my endeavours. The former choice would allow me a pleasant period of virtually freewheeling at the end of an at times hectic career. The latter choice entailed keeping my nose to the grindstone right up to the end, with a rather sudden drop into the void of inactivity.

I chose the way of the workaholic, not really because I could not let go, but on account of the astonishing paucity of literature on the specific problems of very small economic systems. In economic theory as taught in universities all over the world, no proper attention is given to the socio-economic implications of the restrictions of scale encountered in very small societies.

Because the subject is glossed over in all commonly used text books, there is no general awareness even of the existence of this problem field. Neither any urgency to explore it nor any willingness to allocate funds to a project in this field was, to my chagrin, found in the academic circles at home and abroad that I approached in the past years. So, even a very modest book on the outlines of mini-economics might some day come in handy as a building block for a strategy somebody else may develop to break the vicious circle of ignorance and indifference I could not break.

Alas, not much progress under their own steam may be expected from the small number of economists that is personally involved in small economic systems through their jobs. Typically, they are preoccupied myopically in one particular very small society, with a multitude of heterogeneous practical problems, that in larger systems would be shared out to different specialists. Hopping madly from one ad hoc decision to the next, they cannot see the wood for the trees. Snowed under by continuing streams of seemingly unrelated issues, that have to be settled one way or another, with scanty benefit from theoretical guidelines, they are not in a position of sufficient distance to tell systematic from erratic influences, and lack the serenity to turn sneaking suspicions into theories.

Only exceptionally economists, both insiders and outsiders, write anything that may be considered a direct contribution to our general knowledge on the economics of very small societies. This reinforces the vicious circle: because hardly anybody reads about the subject, hardly anybody cares to write about it.

Even though I hold no hopes that this little book will do the trick, it will salve my conscience to know that at least I have done what was within my power to do, in order to advance the view that the subject of mini-economics (which is short for "economics of very small societies") is important enough to merit broad scientific interest. Not only, and not even in the first place, because there are scores of very small countries, confronted on a daily basis with problems that have not come in for their rightful share of academic interest. A stronger reason is that research of the problems of small independent states is bound to shed new light on the economies of peripheral regions in larger economic systems. The most important reason however is that scientific knowledge of the nature and significance of socio-economic scale problems, gained in the 'pure' case of very restricted systems, is most likely to contribute to a much-needed rethinking of economic theory in general, even to the point of triggering a major advance. The case when a national economy is too small and uncomplicated to pose as an abstract entity, cloaked in an ephemeral garb woven of ramshackle macromodels stuffed with aggregate time series, is bound to contribute materially to a healthy suspicion that nations as such are not economic entities, but conglomerates of economic activities, too heterogeneous to offer a sound base for consistent policy making at the national level. From an altogether different angle, a similar view is emerging from recent work of Jane Jacobs. See for instance her fascinating article in The Atlantic Monthly of March 1984. Another herald of a new dawn in social sciences is Fritjof Capra, advancing a holistic approach to replace the Cartesian-Newtonian paradigm: "The qualification of growth and the integration of the notion of scale into economic thought will cause a profound revision of the basic conceptual framework of economics."[1]

At this point I feel obliged to be very frank about the fact that I have accumulated, in many years of empirical research over an unusually wide range, grave doubts about the usefulness of economic theory, as presented in all important contemporary schools of thought. If we pause to think of the vast needs of humanity to run its affairs efficiently with reference to general aims like peace, equity, welfare and continuity, we as economists may well be deeply ashamed of the meagre contributions we have made so far. This point of view has been presented in more detail in an appendix to a previous publication[2], where it may be found by those who really give a damn. I am not bent on proselitizing and mention it only because I have no wish to suppress the fact that I am a dissident in economic thinking.

About the book now. In chapters 2, 3 and 4 I have made use, to a fairly large extent, of what I have written earlier in my thesis[3]. As

1) Capra, F. "The Turning Point", page 236 in the 1983 paperback edition.
2) A.J. Butter "A Road to Full Employment", Amsterdam 1983, ISBN 90 6032 239 8.
3) A.J. Butter "Wat heet onafhankelijk?" (What Price Independence?), Amsterdam 1979 (summary in english).

this was written in my native tongue and the number of copies was restricted, the use of this material here serves the double purpose of making it more accessible, and simplifying my work in preparing the present manuscript. The second chapter is devoted to foreign trade. Chapter 3 deals with the phenomenon of small size in a national economy. In chapter 4 development problems are reviewed. I have hesitated long about, and finally decided against the inclusion of a chapter on transportation and communication. For one thing, because a contract research project on these matters, that I executed in 1978 in the Netherlands Antilles with a too low budget, no assistance in the field work and an incredibly tight time limit, has convinced me that my factual knowledge in this field is far from complete. For another thing, because I did not get around to reading up on it, as there always seem to be higher priorities on my reading list. Finally, but that was an afterthought, shaping itself while the final chapters were written, because the problem of isolation, which is the lack of transportation and communication, is in too many cases inextricably mixed up with the problems of scale in very small societies. An attempt at analytically separating it from scale problems as such is, at the present state of the art, likely to be abortive and might do more harm than good.

Chapter 5 is intended to be a preliminary list of topics for future research, in order to shed much needed light on the interdependence of development problems and the consequences of smallness. It seems plausible that in many respects concomitants of small scale are at the root of deficiencies in development, even to the point that in certain cases development to a selfsustained level is illusory. As some minimal level of livability must be considered a fundamental right of every human being, there is a strong case for international law instead of international charity as a ground for permanent aid that, when development is an unattainable aim, cannot rightly be termed development aid.

This train of thought is further pursued in chapter 6, that, in a way, is the focal chapter of this little book. The basic requirements of livability, subsumed under the concept of viability, whether of humans or human organizations, are seen in their aggregate to constitute a floor to the possibilities of worthwhile human life on earth. There is also a ceiling, as the total of available means within the system is not unlimited. Within this circumscribed realm for human existence a quasi fixed point may be identified, related to a theoretical convergence of a further developed human rights concept to a stable equilibrium of individual rights with the equal rights of all other individuals. In reference to this point a vector of its associated livability requirements may be postulated. Its elements may be taken as proxies for the zero positions on partial scales of development. In reference to the quasi fixed point all interpersonal and intertemporal distribution problems may be mapped in a mutually consistent manner. As any other economic problem may be mapped in terms of its distributional consequences, this opens the road to an operational way of stating common distributional objectives of humanity as touching stones for all plans and actions aimed at personal or group interests, by showing the distributional consequences of any claim on limited resources. Meanwhile, the present state of, and developments in the mundial inequality of wealth, income and power turn the question of the viability of very small states into one that should no longer be evaded.

Chapter 7 closes the book with some attention for recent publications pertaining to the field of mini-economics, some explanations and opinions, and some rather optimistic ideas about what might be achieved in the near and not so near future. Optimism was in order, because pessimism might amount to a self-fulfilling prophesy.

It is a serious shortcoming of this book that references to literature are scanty, to say the least of it. Though the author takes the stand that there simply is not much worthwhile literature on the subject, it is common knowledge that he is not an avid reader, subscribing at times openly to the adagium that what is good in literature is for well over ninety percent just good common sense, with which he thinks he is amply provided himself. Thus he takes it for granted that what is good in his writings is not original and vice versa. The literature consciously used is listed in appendix 1. Appendix 2 lists a number of very small economies. Appendix 3 summarizes my ideas on the possibilities of quasi-cardinal analysis of the interpersonal and intertemporal distribution of welfare in a decomposable mega-model for the Millenium.

The avowed purpose of this book is to engender professional and lay interest in the subject of mini-economics, and to be either a guideline or a stone of offence to those enticed or goaded to take up the subject. It will have missed its purpose if within ten years from now it has not been made redundant by the appearance of at least one better book on mini-economics.

2.

FOREIGN TRADE AND SMALL NATIONS

The economics of international trade deal with "the obstacles that political boundaries raise to the movement of goods, men, money and ideas", as Fabricant[1] succinctly put it. Ricardo, in his days, was thinking of the international movement of goods only when he developed his elegant theory of comparative advantages. Like a fine old lady, even in the most modern garb she manages to retain some of her original elegance, notwithstanding the obvious rift between her and the part of reality she purports to model.

We may take Samuelson's wellknown paraphrasing of the Hekscher-Ohlin model as a fair example. Its modus operandi is relative differences in the availability of factors of production, causing international trade streams. Foreign trade appears as the effect of immobility or restricted mobility of productive forces. In this line of reasoning direct foreign investments, the export of knowhow and migrant labour could replace commodity trade. Increases in the international mobility of money, knowledge and labour would tend to exert a negative influence on the volume of international trade.

A moment's thought should be enough to see that this is contrary to what one should expect. Through increased mobility of production factors, additional production possibilities become economically feasible and are seized in places where this was not possible before on account of local shortages of the factors required. To assume that the newly produced goods would pro tanto replace formerly imported goods, requires the assumptions that the new goods are

1) S. Fabricant "Study of the size and efficiency of the American economy" in: 'The Economic Consequences of the Size of Nations' (ed. A. Robinson), New York 1960, pp. 35-53.

restricted to the home market only, and that for these goods the home market is of a given and constant size. There are no grounds for such assumptions however. On the contrary, one may expect that the average share of new goods, that will enter into international trade, will not differ substantially one way or another from that of other goods already circulating in national and international markets. Moreover the new productions result in new income, equivalent to new effective demand, that will be partly directed toward imported goods. Also, new production households have their own demand for imported inputs, e.g. machinery and raw materials.

If there is any example to be found where increased mobility of production factors did not ultimately result in trade creation instead of trade reduction, that will most certainly not be an example of the general case, but a rare exception. The fundamental flaw of the theory of comparative advantages seems to be that it originates from comparative static partial analysis (i.e. two commodities, two countries), which by one-directional generalisation has become divorced from the dynamics of our multi-directional reality. Ricardo is far easier to forgive for committing this error than the seven or eight generations of economists who, up to this day, failed to correct it.

And yet it has been uncomfortably clear all the time to many of them that the theory fitted the facts very poorly indeed. But, rather amazingly, instead of abandoning their precious paradigm, they did their utmost to make the unruly facts fit it. Differences in education, economies of scale, product life cycles and innovation lags, separately and in combination, were called upon to explain away the discrepancies between the model and reality. For their truly ingenious efforts in these sterile directions I could pay scores of authors my lefthanded compliments. Instead I will only mention Van de Gevel[2], who made a painstakingly good job of listing and dissecting a fair sample of these redecorators of the Old Model.

2) A.J.W. van de Gevel "De proliferatie van modellen van de internationale handel" in: 'De Economist', 119, nr.5, 1971, pp. 556-610.

I am aware that readers, especially those who are in the habit of devoting much of their and their students' time to the post-Ricardian explanation of the international division of labour, may feel that I have been too flippant and offhand in my dismissal of their venerable, almost sacred theory. So exclusively for their benefit I will have another go at it. Those who are already convinced may skip this part.

A rather tautological way of looking at international trade is to focus on the mundial pattern of national surpluses and shortages that is bridged by it. If anywhere, in this pattern the forces shaping international trade should be visible in their effects. From these effects the nature of these forces might be inferred. The old theory amounts to the hypothesis that these forces may be called forces of specialisation and that they *follow* (and not precede) the direction of comparative advantages. But the very nature of some comparative advantages militates against their preceding the associated production pattern. The presence of a labour force meeting the specific requirements of a particular industry could hardly precede the first decision to locate it there. This goes for a lot of other advantages, associated with the growth pole concept.

Still, one might say that these are only particular cases that are insufficient for the falsification of the theory in the general case, and I, for one, would consider that a serious objection. At first sight one might easily think that by empirical research into trade streams and their sources the old theory could once and for all be falsified. Unfortunately matters are considerably less cut and dried. If a research team could not find comparative advantages responsible for a particular international pattern of production and trade, that would in no way amount to a proof that they did not exist or had not existed before. In the same vein, contrary findings would not really support the theory in the absence of proof that the comparative advantages indeed preceded the formation of the associated pattern of national surpluses and shortages. Historical research into the matter would also be necessary to exclude the possibility that not comparative advantages, though present, had induced the producers' decisions at the base of the production pattern, but quite different considerations.

Moreover, in the straightforward empirical approach there seem to be aggregation and desaggregation problems that are difficult to overcome. Only on a high level of abstraction the number of factors considered is small enough for unambiguous conclusions, but these alas apply only to the model and not to reality. If the model's variables are broken down into their component parts, it soon becomes clear that comparative advantages, for instance in the price of labour, are a highly complex matter: under an overall comparative advantage partial disadvantages, even crucial ones, may be concealed. In the opposite case the reverse may be true.

Not only are all economic decision makers confronted at the micro level with their own particular mix of favourable and unfavourable factors, but even if they don't overlook any, they diverge widely in the relative weights they attach to the different factors, and in their attitudes toward uncertainty and risk. As these weightings and attitudes are variable, the same man in virtually the same circumstances may take different decisions at different times. These variations along the time axis are likely to have strong systematic components, for instance through the influence of the mass media. This makes it rather imprudent to regard a times series of aggregate magnitudes as homogeneous in the sense of being based on a stable substratum of consistent economic decision making. Even findings that are statistically significant at some level of probability may point the wrong way.

If empirical research directly aimed at enquiry into the nature and influence of comparative advantages cannot be trusted to prove or disprove the theory we have to look for a different road. One way might be to make up new theories out of whole cloth and set them alongside the old theory, and show that the known facts and maybe a number of common misapprehensions as well, could be explained in ways more satisfactory to the proponents of such new theories. But the new ones might be just as hard to prove as the old one. This approach would multiply instead of solve the problem. So it might be a better idea to stick for the present to the framework of the old theory and inspect it in a formal logical way on the presence of weak spots.

In considering comparative advantages as economic forces we must differentiate between two aspects: what they are and what they do. As to the latter, we might for instance say that they influence the unit costs of production, but it would be erroneous to say in the same general sense that they influence the dispositions of economic decision makers. A policy maker, both at the macro and the micro level, may not be aware of certain advantages or disadvantages, or may deem them too insignificant. In other cases he may find himself restricted to only some options, that are for all practical purposes indifferent to them. Many other factors may be considered weightier than production cost differentials at a particular moment. Other factors than comparative advantages may decide the location and production choices of production households. To which extent this is possible depends at least in part on the way in which comparative advantages and disadvantages are defined.

If any influence at all in favour of one location (or production basket) over another would be called a comparative advantage, there could be no other factors left. Such a definition would, however, turn any amount of factors normally regarded as extra-economical into economic ones. This would set us the task, inter alia, of weighting matters like political ambitions, family ties, status seeking and lust for adventure against labour and capital differentials. Setting such wide limits to the problem field could hardly be called economic analysis in the customary sense. Clearly, being economists we must favour a narrower definition of comparative advantages.

The mere fact that we do so has as its corollary that the set of other factors influencing the international allocation pattern is not an empty set. This means that the good old theory can at the very best offer a partial explanation.

We might choose a definition excluding only all non-economic influences. That definition would not offer any discrimination *within* the field of economics and thus would be spurious from a methodological point of view.

A definition of comparative advantages that could be of any use in economic analysis must be of such a nature that the set of economic forces excluded from it is not empty. This strengthens the conclusion that the old theory, if not altogether false, is at least sorrily incomplete.

A workable definition of comparative advantages might label as such all factors, and only those, that influence the comparative costs of production, Economic factors excluded from this definition are, logically, those influencing yields and those that, influencing neither costs nor yields, might yet be relevant to the allocation process. Whether any factors of this third category actually exist is not crucial to the present line of reasoning, and for all I care we may assume that this set is empty as long as none of its elements is identified.

So there are in any case two sets of relevant economic factors. Our next concern is whether these sets are disjunct. The answer is easy. Changes in production prices often lead to changes in selling prices, so there is bound to be an overlap. The conjunction of both sets cannot be empty.

We will take a closer look now at one element, any element from this subset. For the moment we disregard all possible higher order effects springing from interaction between different elements. We look only at the direct effect on costs and yields that is caused by a change in the selected element. This boils down to a ceteris paribus position in which there are no changes in country B and changes both in costs and yields in country A.

If the change in costs is opposite to the change in yields, the changes reinforce one another. Explanation in terms of comparative costs points the right way, but overestimates its force. It may even be wrong though, if the effect is too weak to transcend some transom value required for the induction of changes in the pattern of trade between A and B.

If the changes in costs and yields parallel one another their combined effect is weakened and may point either way. This makes for a number of possible casus positions.

I am not going to spell them out, as to me and probably most of us as well this approach is extremely boring. But to point out their existence was not superfluous: it served to locate a good number of holes in the theory and has implicitly offered a broader framework of analysis that is more likely to hold water. This, however, is outside the scope of this book. It will entail a great mass of empirical research, not just into patterns of international trade, but also in the history of national sectors of production and their recent development as, for instance, may be made explicit by shift and share analysis techniques, currently used by regional economists.

It is hardly to be expected that the results of this type of research would point towards specialisation, moreover caused mainly by relative cost advantages. For instance, in Latin America agrarian export surpluses are in a number of cases relatively cheap at the cost of a pauperised rural work force. To call this a comparative advantage is stretching the meaning of the term too far, not just from a moral point of view, but because it is a matter of record that pauperism and virtual slavery make for economically inefficient production structures. In Latin America this is corroborated by evaluations of the goals of agrarian decision makers. Too often they do not seek increases of their economic gains, which are more than ample already, but the maintenance of their status and power, to which end they even oppose the adoption of efficient new techniques or cultivation of larger parts of their domains. Read for instance what Harrison[3] has written on the latifundio and minifundio.

Some authors broke new ground. In Van de Gevel's review article mention is also made of the 'unorthodox' theory of Linder, which roughly amounts to the thesis that international trade is to be explained by the same causes that determine trade flows not crossing national boundaries. Monopolistic competition catering to buyer

3) P. Harrison "Inside the Third World", Pelican 1979.

idiosyncracies may, according to this author, cause flourishing bilateral trade in near-identical commodities. "Ships bringing European beer to Milwaukee take American beer to Europe. The strong elements of monopolistic competition should be incorporated into trade theory as a trade-creating force." From this example I infer that Linder is not an accomplished beer drinker, as he appears to be utterly insensitive to the worlds of difference between a bottle of Carlsberg and a can of Budweiser. Nevertheless, his argument is sound enough, though it does not help us to understand what is so special about *international* trade.

An other theory that cannot be called 'orthodox', developed by Raoul Prebish, has been given a fair rendering by Aleman[4] in a formal model. It pivots on lack of symmetry in the trade relationships between developed (center) and underdeveloped nations (periphery), causing a secular deterioration of the terms of trade for the latter group. The alleged effect of this mechanism, as claimed by adherents to this theory, is a transfer of income from poor to rich nations.

Now the concept of terms of trade is a rather confusing one, as it may be defined in at least three clearly different ways. For instance, figures referring to the barter terms of trade have more than once been used to bolster an argument on the incomes terms of trade. Also, commodity prices used in the calculations were, in several cases, not producers' prices, but wholesale prices at central markets, e.g. London, and thus inclusive of freights etcetera. By this expedient a sharp fall in freight rates could be made to look like a fall in raw commodity prices relative to the f.o.b. prices of manufactures, amounting to an apparent deterioration of the barter terms of trade for primary producers.

Both on empirical and theoretical grounds the Prebish thesis comes in for serious criticism on several counts, as has been argued by,

4) R.T. Aleman "Die Theorie der peripherischen Wirtschaft" in: 'Weltwirtschaftliches Archiv', 1955 pp. 9 and following.

inter alia, Viner[5], Baldwin[6] and Haberler[7]. Still, it has many adherents, as it offers developing nations a good platform in negotiations with developed nations. A case in point is UNCTAD I, held at Geneva in 1964. Friedeberg[8] has given a detailed account of it and its background.

No doubt many criticisms of the Prebish doctrine are valid, as its theory is rather shaky, but their impact lacks force, since they come from supporters of the old paradigm, which is not very robust either. Meanwhile, it was only to be expected that attempts would be forthcoming to give this, from a political angle so opportune, theory more solid underpinnings, and possibly even put her to use in the east-west controversy.

To a certain extent, Emmanuel[9] has managed to do just that with his "theory of unequal exchange" This theory is based on international wage differentials. It entails a high degree of abstraction and is unsatisfactory in its dealing with the heterogeneity of labour, which is at least one significant reason of international wage differences. Emmanuel's alleged imperialistic inequalities in the exchange of commodities are biased and may be explained equally unsatisfactory as transformations of the international heterogeneity of labour.

If there are any other theories of international trade that amount to anything, I must have missed them. To be quite frank, I have not sought very exhaustively, because never for a single moment have I entertained the thought that a general theory of international trade could be of any use in the particular case that made me enter this field: the Netherlands Antilles.

5) J. Viner "International Trade and Economic Development" Oxford 1953.
6) R.E. Baldwin "Secular movements in the terms of Trade", in 'American Economic Review', May 1955.
7) G. Haberler "Terms of trade and economic development" in: 'Economic Development for Latin America' (ed. H.S. Ellis), London 1961.
8) A.S. Friedeberg "The United Nations Conference on Trade and Development of 1964" Rotterdam 1970 2nd.ed.
9) A. Emmanuel "L'échange inégal", Paris 1969.

All such theories describe, in one way or another, relationships between aggregated magnitudes. If the aggregates are unstable even the best theory is of no avail. For stable aggregates a much larger statistical mass is needed than can be provided by the import and export transactions of a nation with less than a quarter of a million inhabitants. These rather small figures remain, moreover, well within any reasonable margin of error of world trade totals, so there is no point in comparisons of these widely differing magnitudes. Even if this were not so, and a theoretical model could meaningfully be quantified with the proper statistical data, the knowledge thus gained would be of academic interest only, as it would be futile if not downright suicidal for a very small nation to attempt to influence its trade partners by a consistent trade policy all its own and not adapted ad hoc from its more powerful neighbours.

Thus I did not waste any time on theories of foreign trade in the Antilles project, but later on, when turning the research report into a doctor's thesis[10], I had to be less casual about it. So I read up on the subject and was quite pleased to find that also from a theoretical angle I had been right not to go by the book.

For all trade theories, no matter how widely they may differ in other respects, have one thing in common: they are models of the interaction between the productive and distributive mechanisms of different economies. If in one of those economies these mechanisms are absent or too rudimentary to transmit the effects they are supposed to transmit, these theories are bound to break down. And indeed, there are economies where the forces of the market are too weak or insufficiently integrated to produce the effects theories ascribe to them. Very small island economies are cases in point, but there are other examples as well. This view is supported by several authors.

"Some economists, myself included, have argued that the economic

10) A.J. Butter "Wat heet onafhankelijk?" ('What Price Independence?'), Amsterdam 1979.

models constructed to describe the working of industrial economies (for example the Keynesian model) are not necessarily, or even probably, suitable for exporters of primary products, because their fundamental assumptions do not apply. They are misleading as a way of thinking about such an economy; they lead to the wrong policy conclusions; it would be better not to use them in the main courses on economic principles in the universities of such countries because they do not prepare students for their future work."

This opinion of Seers[11] with reference to economies mainly supported by the export of raw commodities, is with a slightly different approach also supported by Wallich[12] . The main argument for this line of thought is found in the incomplete and one-sided production structure of such economies: they just have to be wide open, without anything of the niceties of equilibrating mechanisms in the international division of labour, which according to the orthodox theory further the approach to an optimum and according to newer theories lead in the opposite direction.

Raw commodities producers are only one class of open economies not showing the pattern assumed by most theorists. Seers' opinion also holds for other nations with a fragmentary structure of their economies, no matter whether they fall inside or outside the group of less developed nations. Specialisation due to international trade can only mean a process of change from a less specialised to a more specialised production structure. If changes do not lead in this direction or even away from it, all theories explicitly or implicitly pivoting on the mechanism of specialisation are illegitimate.

Why do economies with a fragmentary production structure exist? In a number of cases we find that a traditional and 'backward' pre-Newtonian society, with hardly any foreign trade, has been opened up from outside. In other cases there are no roots in local non-

11) D. Seers "The mechanism of an open petroleum economy", in: 'Social and Economic Studies', June 1964 p. 233.
12) H.C. Wallich "Monetary Problems of an Export Economy", Harvard 1950.

Western cultures: they did not exist or were completely wiped out and all we find is a relatively young settlement with an economic structure that has been lopsided and fragmentary right from the start. There may be other types. Often matters have been aggravated by the one-sided development of a single sector with an enclave character.

For the purpose of this chapter, there is no need to go much deeper into this. Many economies are of such a scale and complexity of structure, that their statistics can be fitted to models explaining foreign trade by the interplay of their endogeneous economic forces with those within the economies of their trade partners. In such cases it may be hard to decide whether or not these models come passably close to reality. But there are also open economies, lacking either or both the necessary scale and complexity, where such endogeneous forces are absent or too weak, because the national production structure is too fragmentary for the proper transmission of impulses from one sector to another. In those cases models based on the interplay of economic forces are not valid.

In all likelihood, at present there simply is no theory that offers a satisfactory explanation of the trade with or between nations that have incomplete and fragmentary production structures. The defective mechanism to be blamed for this unsatisfactory situation is an old acquaintance of economists, generally assumed to be around in the guise of the Invisible Hand: the allocation mechanism. The failure of this mechanism is at the back of the fact, observed by Seers and others, that in some economies our models break down. Approaching the matter from a different angle, this has been observed also by Van Philips[13] : "In an underdeveloped export economy (. . .) the dynamic forces originate in foreign trade, but their favourable effect largely ebbs back into foreign trade. The underdeveloped and incoherent economic structure and its low degree of diversification cause a favourable external incentive to be absorbed

13) P.A.M. van Philips "Public Finance and Less Developed Economy, with Special Reference to Latin America", The Hague 1957.

to a relatively small degree." The author refers here to characteristics of a stage of development. But in other cases fragmentary economic structures may be identified where the weaknesses are not temporal aspects of their development, but the consequences of structural factors, not amenable to change. The Netherlands Antilles may be seen as an example of such an economy. Both its area and its labour force are too small to afford the physical base for a fairly complete and integrated production structure. These and other factors limiting the scope of very small economies will be discussed in the next chapter.

3.

SMALL AND VERY SMALL ECONOMIES

Literature on the economic implications of the size of nations is not very abundant. Only in micro-economics and business administration there is a coherent tradition of analysis of scale problems, but on aggregate levels the subject has come in for attention only in a haphazard way. I have yet to come across the first macro-economic text book dealing with the theoretical implications of differences in the absolute size between various economies, though this subject is certainly important enough to merit attention. Possibly this near-blind spot in the state of the art has been caused by the leading position of American text books in this field: American economists are, at home, typically not confronted with the constraints that are relevant to very small markets.

So it is maybe not so surprising that in the scattered sources dealing with the subject the term 'small economy' has no precise meaning, but is used only in a relative sense. Some authors regard Canada and Australia as small nations and of course Earth is only a small planet compared to Jupiter. But it is hardly likely that restrictions of scale relevant to, say, Barbados have the same relevance to Denmark or New Zealand. So if small nations in general may be taken as nations with less than 15 million inhabitants, I would like to add, by way of distinction, the term 'very small economy' to designate societies with populations less than one million. In the following pages I have used this term or its paraphrases where it seemed expedient to exclude the possibility that observations referring to such very small economies might too easily be thought relevant also for economies ten or twenty times as large. This demarcation line at the one million level is, I admit, wholly arbitrary. But it will have to serve as long as there is no quantitative analysis available of the various relevant aspects, that would afford a better base for some other classification of size.

Maybe for some analytic purposes, not population, but the total land surface, land area weighted for economic potential or the national product might be a better indicator of size. But also in this case there are no criteria to do this in a non-arbitrary way. For the present we will stick to the use of population size as a yardstick, not forgetting however that in a time series analysis it is at the same time one of the variables to be considered.

One of the few economists who have intensively and over a long period occupied themselves with scale problems on aggregate levels is Kohr[1]. In this field he ranks as a pioneer, though there is plenty to be said against his vision on the optimal size of an economy. Above all, he is eager to make readers share his conviction that all sorts of problems that are nowadays found in our modern societies have their roots mainly in a long term historical development towards ever larger national and supranational economic systems. As a result of this preoccupation his verbal analysis is rather onesided and manages to bypass completely the predicaments of very small economic systems, even though in his very thesis that there is an optimal size for an economy, sub-optimality is implied for the smaller ones. So Kohr's book was, though quite interesting in itself, not in the least helpful for the matter in hand.

More was to be expected at first sight from the papers of a conference held in 1957 in Lisbon by The International Economic Association on "The Economic Consequences of the Size of Nations"[2]. Under this title the papers and proceedings of the conference, edited by Robinson, were published three years later. Among the other well-known participants were celebrities like Fabricant, Kuznets, Scitovsky and Triffin. That even these prominent authors had little or nothing to say that was noteworthy in relation to very small economic systems may be blamed on two causes. First: their main focus was on the question whether very large economies had access

1) L. Kohr "The Overdeveloped Nations", Swansea 1976.
2) E.A.G. Robinson (ed.) "The Economic Consequences of the Size of Nations", London 1960.

to economies of scale that were out of reach for smaller, yet sizable nations. Second: as empirical data in this field were (and are) rather scarce, the authors had to make too many assumptions and were, to my taste, in a number of cases not very fortunate in doing so.

But after this disappointment I had a lucky break when in a second-hand bookshop I came across a modest little book. The institute of Commonwealth Studies of the University of London had held a two-year seminar, which started in October 1962, on the problems of very small nations "... to investigate these problems and to attempt to discover how far there were problems common to all small territories."

There were more than twenty papers from different authors but the resulting publication, that appeared in 1967 under editorship of Benedict[3], contained only ten. Of these, five are rather general, respectively from an economic, sociological, demographic, administrative and political point of view. The other five are case studies. The papers left out of the book are also case studies. Amongst those are three that deal with Caribbean islands and may be rather relevant to our subject, but they were not available. As readers may be luckier in unearthing these papers than I was, I will list them here.

1. D.J. Morgan 'The West Indies'
2. D. Lowenthal 'Montserrat: autonomy in microcosmos'
3. N. Harrigan 'The Virgin Islands: a case study in smallness'.

Kuznets[4] has presented data illustrating that, generally, both in rich and in poor countries foreign trade tends to be larger in relation to national income as population size gets smaller. One might expect this to be so, because the smaller the economy, the smaller also the chance of a near-complete and well-balanced set of natural resources within its national borders. However, this is only one of the possible causes. An important constraint at the low end of the scale of na-

3) B. Benedict (ed.) "Problems of Smaller Territories", London 1967.
4) S. Kuznets 'Economic growth of small nations' in: "The Economic Consequences of the Size of Nations" (ed. E.A.G. Robinson), London 1960.

tions is also the absolute size of its work force, which severely restricts the scope for differentiation within the labour market. The smaller a national labour market, the higher are the frictons caused by segmentation. This puts a brake on the proliferation of trades and professions that is a corollary to differentiation and expansion of the production structure. Labour then becomes a bottleneck and restricts the set of commodities that can be home-produced.

In a country with a small territory the impossibility of selfsupport in a number of raw materials will most probably be an important trade-creating force. But there are also countries that, though small in population size, have fairly large territories and are not too bad off in factor endowments. Here we find an other constraint in operation: low average population density at the root of high costs per head for infrastructure and transportation. The great internal distances also aggravate the frictions in the labour market. This is notably the case when there are geographical barriers effectively splitting it up. For instance, if a territory consists of a number of islands. The Netherlands Antilles have the worst of it in the Caribbean: their very small territory is distributed over two groups of three islands that are wide apart, which means that their internal transport distances are way out of proportion to their size.

A further constraint for the development of the production structure may be a scarcity of good locations, either through scarcity of suitable land or because of a too small recruiting area for the work force. This aspect may be particularly important in the case of foreign private investment, if a choice is to be made between locations in different countries. In the Caribbean, possibly also in other parts of the world, this has led to an unholy competition between governments, trying to outdo one another in the offering of tax incentives.
This futile attempt to compensate for a lack of real locational advantages has meanwhile escalated to a fairly important incomes transfer from poor to rich countries, for which they can only blame themselves and one another.

Michaely[5] has pointed out that, the smaller the country, both the number of important trade partners and the number of commodities entering into the trade in sizeable quantities tend to be lower. His conclusions are based on averages for groups of countries and may be influenced by the fact that in the world more small than large nations are, economically, satellites to a neighbour. Though they were not included in his sample, the Netherlands Antilles seem to fit Michaely's description and show a fairly high concentration both in trade partners and in commodities.

In the export from less developed countries Michaely found, contrary to expectations, the highest concentration index for goods in the group of the larger countries. Knox[6] has tried to explain this by saying that "the degree of economic diversification is affected by the degree of development as well as by a country's size. . . . Thus among these underdeveloped countries we have conflicting forces: large size makes for diversified exports while economic backwardness makes for concentration." This explanation boils down to the hypothesis that in Michaely's samples the larger less developed countries were, on an average, more backward than the smaller ones. It seems imperative that in further research on these matters some proxy for the level of development should be introduced in the models, for weighting the results of estimations.

Often it is taken for granted that in international trade small countries have a handicap compared to bigger ones, because of their size. In the role of sellers they will hardly ever be monopolists or even one of the larger oligopolists. Neither can they be important buyers. This would adversely affect prices, buying frequencies and delivery lags. Knox even has it that ". . . a small country cannot influence the prices of its exports or its imports, and thus has to bear transport costs on both."

5) M. Michaely 'Concentration of imports and exports: an international comparison' in: "Economic Journal", December 1958.
6) A.D. Knox 'Some economic problems of small countries' in: "Problems of Smaller Territories" (ed. B. Benedict), London 1967.

I disagree there. Trade, in general, is not conducted between governments, but between private firms in an international field with wide open competition. So it is hardly probable that some firm in a large country could have more market power than a firm in a smaller country, only for that reason. Moreover, there is the widely spread phenomenon of price discrimination between home and foreign markets, caused by producers wanting to run their production lines at full or near-full capacity. Exporters and importers all over the world make it their business to be well aware of the possibilities this offers for their gain. It is far from unusual that for a certain product the local wholesale price exceeds the f.o.b. export price. Especially a small country, with an incomplete production structure, may profit from this situation, because it does not have to protect its own nonexistent producers from unfair foreign competition and dumping. Furthermore, transport costs are always borne by the buyer, who would be exempt of them by receiving the goods at the point of sale and carrying them home on his back.

Whoever, from some first-hand knowledge of the exporting and importing business, is aware how wide generalisations as the one above from Knox may be off the mark, will certainly not be impressed by the armchair reflections of Prachowny[7]. This author manages, on the first page of his book, to move in a direction leading far from reality, by his choice of a definition for his subject: "A small open economy is any country (or other political jurisdiction, for that matter) that treats the price of any internationally traded commodity or asset as exogeneously determined and attempts to maximize some objective function with this constraint in mind."

This is a nice example of the pure scientific approach. The scientist has the freedom, or shall we say 'Narrenfreiheit', to make his own definitions and he is to be praised for the exclusion of misunderstandings, by making them fully explicit. Unluckily however, in reality it is utterly impossible to identify prices that can be regarded

7) M.F.J. Prachowny "Small Open Economies", Lexington/Toronto/London 1975.

as given for any country at all. Possibly with the exception of rare monopoly goods, for any internationally traded good buyers may make their choice from a range of prices for near-identical and even identical commodities. Often, but by no means always, such price differences are associated with real or imaginary differences in the qualities of the goods or in the conditions of sale. Every importer, and even in a very small country there are bound to be several of them, will make his own selection from this field. In making this choice the price he will have to pay is less important than his prospects of gain on the deal. It is not true that those prospects are inversely correlated to import prices. In the case when an importer has some grip on his distribution channels in the home market, which may be easier in a small than in a large system, he may stand to gain more from expensive imports than from their cheaper substitutes. If the government attempts to regulate consumer prices of foreign goods by regulating the profit margins in wholesale price calculations, as is the case in the Netherlands Antilles, there is even an incentive for importers not to buy cheap. However, that has nothing to do with exogeneous market power as Prachowny has it.

One might think that small open economies would, on an average, be worse off than larger ones, because in the field of prices, qualities and sales conditions they would have only second choice. Even that assumption, far less extreme than the one adopted by Prachowny, is not acceptable, as long as there is not a shred of hard evidence to back it up.

Prachowny has wisely put himself out of reach for these and similar citicisms, by explicitly eliminating economic reality: "This study is strictly theoretical and abstract in nature. It deals with a hypothetical small open economy. No attempt is made to cope with the practical implications of the analysis for any particular country that may approximate the characteristics of an SOE." (SOE meaning small open economy – AJB).

Indeed it will not be simple to find, among the many widely differing small economies in this world, even one case roughly corresponding to this author's model. Moreover, the model has a structure that cannot be quantified properly for very small economies. The meaningful use of macro-economics, if at all possible, presupposes the existence of stable aggregates. But stability is lacking when the statistical mass is too small and the law of large numbers does not apply.

On top of this, the model is based on the Hekscher-Ohlin theorem of relative factor endowments, that is not valid in fractionally structured small economies, where the allocation mechanism is without force. So policy makers had better leave this model where it belongs: up in the air.

At this junction, however, the author commits a methodological sin. A scientist is within his rights when he constructs a wholly abstract model, and even points out that it is divorced from reality. But if one does this, there is no logical ground left to claim, at the same time, practical relevance for it. Prachowny seems to be blissfully unaware of this when he writes: "Although the SOE is a theoretical proposition, it is not devoid of empirical relevance. There are a large number of countries that more fully satisfy the specifications of an SOE than they do the models of larger, or essentially closed economies." How anyone can be so sanguine about this, without ". . . any attempt to cope with the practical implications of the analysis for any particular country . . ." beats me altogether. But Prachowny even lists a number of examples, apparently plucked from the air: Austria, Belgium, Canada, Denmark, The Netherlands and New Zealand. This clears up one point anyway: the author is dealing with a different class of 'small' economies than the ones that are the focus of interest of the present book. So we will leave this blind alley and return to our subject.

Noteworthy is the unfavourable position of very small countries in the matter of non-tradeables, which are commodities normally not entering into foreign trade for technical reasons or because of prohibitive costs and/or risks of transportation. Home production of such goods may be necessary, also in cases where the small scale of production, for the very small home market only, causes the unit price to be much higher than elsewhere.

This is of great relevance in the case of collective and quasi-collective goods. The proper supply of even minimal government, education and health services may represent such a heavy drain on the resources of a very small country that it obviates financial viable independence. Micronesia is probably the most extreme example.

The other side of this leaden medal is that in very small countries it is not unusual that goods are imported that rank as non-tradeables elsewhere. If through lack of the proper mineral endowments certain building materials, for instance roof tiles, have to be imported, this may be of little or no consequence for the price of subsidized low-budget housing, as it is generally possible to use cheaper substitutes for too expensive imports. But in private and business building such materials acquire an enhanced snob appeal, boosting the demand. This causes an additional need for foreign exchange, that has no counterpart in countries large or lucky enough not to be faced with a similar effective import demand. This amounts to a real disadvantage in foreign trade: any circumstance contributing to the demand for foreign exchange causes additional pressure on the external value of the national monetary unit.

From what was said above it should be clear that the set of commodities labeled 'non-tradeable' may show marked differences from one country to another and from one period to the next. Relevant factors making for this latitude of content of the term are: the removal or raising of barriers to home production, the prices and properties of substitutes, changes in the costs of transportation, handling and insurance and, finally, changes in the price of and the effective demand for these commodities. These factors are interdependent.

The trade barrier of transportation and handling costs works both ways, but may be of different height for imports and exports, as between two ports the freight rates and risks of damage to the cargo may be different either way. If in a port a high proportion of the incoming goods comes in containers, whereas the outgoing freight is preponderantly of the mass goods type, it stands to reason that the outgoing container rates will be lower than the incoming ones. Discrepancies between total tonnages coming in and going out and differences in the types of vessels required also make for differentials in the rates. Differences in insurance costs are likely when in a port the risk of pilfering is substantially higher for imports than for exports. This factor is relevant to ports in the Netherlands Antilles.

Trade barriers, even if they are not prohibitive, are handicaps in foreign markets and favour home production. In a very small home market this advantage may be outweighed by the restriction of production techniques to those fitting a small volume of production. In a dynamic context this makes for instability. Rising costs of labour, the stagnation of techniques and the lack of scope for growth through higher efficiency may at any point of the business cycle push firms into the red. Infant industries are especially likely to get crushed if they are not heavily protected. But protection makes it too easy for them to make local consumers pay through the nose for their inefficiencies. We will go into this later as I found it to be quite relevant in a case I studied, which made me understand how in very small economies the protection of import substituting industries may turn into a form of economic suicide.

Industrial producers in a small country may have a quite serious disadvantage compared to their collegues elsewhere as the difference in size of the home market may increase the dependence on exports. Even when a fall in exports is no immediate threat to the continuity of a firm, the producer in a small market carries an added risk, because disturbances of a given intensity are much sharper felt, because of their weight relative to total sales, which increases as the size of the market gets smaller. Also the physical possibilities to make up for adversities by increased sales efforts may be severely restricted.

Governments of very small nations are generally well aware of such threats to employment. Their political aversion to social unrest following lay-offs may give them an unhealthy eagerness to eliminate entrepreneurial risks, by affording protection against foreign competition. They habitually cover this up with the 'infant industry' argument. This, however, is only applicable to temporal risks that have to be weathered, and not to the structural disadvantages indicated here.

Improper use of protection breeds inefficiency and, through inflated consumer prices, leads to a barely hidden subsidy of marginal jobs and, worse, marginal employers. Social policies are an admitted necessity for any government, but to disguise them as economic policies is wrong, as this is ultimately a dead end. Even not so small economies, like The Netherlands, would be better off if their governments took this to heart.

There are many commodities in effective demand that cannot be produced efficiently within a very small economy, and hence have to be imported. The less complete and more fragmentary the production structure, the higher will be the import fraction in total spending. Especially in a period of expanding national income, a very small country is hard put to generate the amount of foreign exchange to cover a rising need for it. Attempts to reduce the demand for imports are by and large futile. Thus there is great pressure to find new sources of foreign income and to expand existing ones. One way would be export growth, but in a very small country this possibility is often restricted, not only by lack of investment funds, but also by the bottleneck of a too small labour market. An other obstacle to export growth, mentioned by Nurkse[8], concerns the reactions of foreign producers to new competition in their home markets. This view, notwithstanding its faint air of comparative statics, has its merits. But here a very small country may have the advantage. The disturbances created by its entry in a foreign market will have to be of a certain order of magnitude, relative to the size of that market, to cause sharp reactions from competitors. Their impact must be heavier yet to goad foreign governments into increased protection. Even so, a very small nation offers only a minuscule target for retaliation and the use of heavy artillery to squash gnats is frowned upon in international relationships. For the very small there may be a margin of freedom to creep through the seams of the system, as long as they do not overplay their hands.

As to types of new economic activity in very small economies, it is

8) R. Nurkse "Patterns of Trade and Development", Stockholm 1959.

not likely that these will be innovations, because they lack the scope to develop new techniques and new capabilities endogeneously. Depending on the geographical situation, there may be an accent on firms and products in the expansion phase of their life cycles, when production nearer to growing markets is rational.

Other newcomers may be relocating full grown and senescing industries, eager to profit from low wages, legal, fiscal and any other advantages a new location may have to offer. In relocations we find push before pull. Decision makers become progressively aware of the drawbacks of their actual situations before diagnosing them as locational disadvantages, to be overcome by relocating somewhere else. Only then they start shopping around for a new place and can its lures be of influence. Entrepreneurs are not omniscient and the information at their disposal is centered around their actual operations.

Incomplete knowledge also influences the potential buyers of new products. With commodities frequently traded in sizeable quantities, not judged by trade marks but by the certified properties of samples, this is far less important than it is with differentiated consumer goods. Knox points this out in the paper that was already cited. He concludes that new producers of raw commodities will have less trouble finding new markets than new producers of individualised final goods. This however goes only for new trade marks. It does not hold for goods newly produced through licensing under existing brand names, and is only partly valid if importers or large distributors sell the new products under their own labels, substituting them for similar former imports from other producers. Thus changes in the origin of canned goods may hardly be noticed by the final consumers.

About yet another aspect of incomplete knowledge, Knox remarks ". . . that investors are mainly influenced by the market they know well and this is generally the market of their own country. The range of potential investments is thus likely to be greater where the home market is large than where it is small."

I disagree with him for two good reasons. The range of final goods sold in small national markets is practically the same as that in larger ones. The very fact that many of those goods are imported is an incentive to ponder on the possibilities of local production. In fact, it frequently happens this way. Initiatives come quite often from importers hoping to improve their gains. It is not rare to see them start off importing in bulk and repacking for retailing, saving mainly on freights, and subsequently integrating further stages of the production processes.

The second objection against Knox's statement concerns investment money. A small open economy is likely to be also wide open to capital movements. Resident individuals, firms and institutions are, by analogy to Knox's argument, only too well aware of the risks of home investments, so precious little of the savings finds its way into local ventures. The remainder is put away in real estate or leaks abroad. Typically, risk bearing investments are financed by foreign businessmen. Their frame of reference, more often than not, is a large home market. This would pull the wrong way if Knox was right.

An important disadvantage of a small market, that is overlooked too often, is its predisposition for a monopolistic structure. This may easily be evident in the structure of its importing business, but possibly the clearest example is to be found in the case when just one factory is sufficient to meet home demand of one or more commodities, without the prospect of finding export markets. A second factory would be redundant. In such cases labour and management, in turn or together, may deftly use the fear of government for social unrest through lay-offs, to obtain protection. And increases of protection when prices have to be raised to accomodate higher wages. As more and more industries fit themselves snugly under this umbrella, it becomes progressively harder for the government to refuse such preferential treatment to others. In the wake of this development we find consumers paying inflated prices for poor quality, compared to the alternative of unhindered imports. The matter is aggravated by the fact that type variations in the products are largely suppressed, because otherwise the production runs would become too small. The treacherous toilet paper produced in Curacao is an example of consumer misery caused by protection.

But there is more to it. No government can afford to give its protection and be done with it. By affording protection it puts itself under the obligation to mitigate the disadvantages of monopoly. It has to institute price control and active supervision of the quality and regular availability of the protected items. The necessarily small administrative apparatus of a very small country may become completely snowed under by such activities, hardly leaving time for other matters. I have observed this a number of times when visiting the Department of Economic Affairs of the Netherlands Antilles and this has given me a great admiration for the virtuosity and lightning speed of its harassed executives in providing ad hoc answers to complicated questions from their ministers and other members of the body political. Such a situation cannot be conducive to good government.

Possibly worse yet is the fact that through protection the already very weak market mechanism is completely suppressed and its signals are distorted or muted altogether. A small government lacks the scope to set up proper mechanisms to monitor the economy. So it has to go practically without proper observation, analysis, planning and control in its attempts to steer an economy that has been put out of reach of 'the invisible hand'. It is, when all is said and done, a stupid and near-suicidal thing to create the need for more and more control where the possibilities for control are structurally absent to a very large extent.

From a sociological angle it is important that smallness of a society leads to the preponderance of a rather special type of relationship. As Benedict[9] put it: "... because of the smallness of the total social field, many roles are played by relatively few individuals ... The same individuals are brought into contact over and over again in various activities."

9) B. Benedict 'Social aspects of smallness' in "Problems of Smaller Territories" (ed. B. Benedict), London 1967.

This multiplicity of social relationships strongly influences conduct and decisions of the actors: impersonal and rational standards are modified by personal motives. A man in such a society is not judged by his acts, but by his birth and influence. Following Max Weber and Talcott Parsons, Benedict uses the concepts 'particularism' and 'universalism' to contrast this type of behaviour, particular to communities where practically nobody is an outsider, to the rational and unpersonal behaviour, that is required in modern economic life. As the author remarks, "A shopkeeper should treat all his customers alike or a doctor all his patients. The roles are functionally specific." Universalistic relationships are affectively neutral, whereas particularistic relationships are charged by often strong positive and negative sentiments.

Knox[10] remarks: "It is a commonplace that economic development requires at times a good deal of social change. It requires the acceptance by a people at large of the need for adjustment. It may well be that small countries have a greater social cohesiveness to help them in this task." But Benedict is much less sanguine about this. In the first place, ". . . a strong network of particularistic relationships does not mean social harmony . . . The intense factionalism of small communities is a matter of repeated observation . . ."

The second caveat, considered to be more serious, is that in economic development achievements must be based on rational standards, and for this function-specific roles are required. "The affective component must be as neutral as possible, or rational choice in terms of efficiency of the enterprise becomes impossible. We are familiar with these problems even in large-scale societies, but in such societies there are always possibilities of bringing in outsiders. The social field is large enough to permit this. In small-scale societies there are no outsiders."

As an outside observer, one does not have to be a professional sociologist to become soon painfully aware of the quite serious economic implications of the fact that in a very small society every-

10) A.D. Knox 'Some economic problems of small countries' in: "Problems of Smaller Territories" (ed. B. Benedict), London 1967.

body knows everybody else, and often quite well at that. The execution of consistent economic policies, in itself far from easy in the absence of a workable differentiation between micro and macro levels, attains additional pitfalls for decision makers who are in permanent personal contact with the individuals affected by their dispositions. Politicians and government executives alike may rest assured that evenhandedness and integrity in the performance of their jobs will be punished by the loss of friends and the acquisition of bitter enemies, and that these petty accounts will come up for settlement whenever they meet their 'victims' in other social roles. Under such conditions universalistic conduct even becomes inefficient as the perpetrator will soon be ostracised. The politician will not be re-elected and the official, if not fired, will be moved to a position where he can do not further 'harm'. Very small economies find themseves in a predicament here that is not shared by larger ones.

Offhand it appears to be rather probable that the social psychology of particularistic behaviour shows a parallel with that of a fairly well mapped area of relationships within business and other organisations: the interface between higher and lower hierarchical levels. To be one of the boys and one of the bosses at the same time makes for a rather stereotyped brand of stress, that may bring one's behaviour at cross purposes with the aims of the organization. Here also we come across 'irrationality' in terms of efficiency, which yet may be taken by the individual as a normal effort to find a rational compromise between conflicting roles. The parallel does not stop there. A person prey to role conflicts in the small social field of a firm is subject to tensions that will in time be detrimental to the level of his performance, detracting from his job satisfaction and personal happiness. The stress may become a drain on his health and even kill him in the end. It stands to reason that, likewise, conflicting social roles in the particularistic setting of a very small society are burdening their victims from cradle to grave with stress. This is a particularly vicious drawback of mini-societies. I predict that its effects can be found in vital statistics and health records of very smal nations, by a cross section analysis.

There is more to be said about the predicament of the individual caught between the demands of conflicting roles. One hypothesis could be that personalistic acts, in which a decision maker shows his awareness of the fact that he needs leeway also in his other roles in a small social field, could yet be termed rational acts, in terms of a stable compromise between the different roles. I do not think that this is true, and presently I will try to explain why I think that personalistic decision making is not rational in the Cartesian sense.

If I am right about this, it means that in mini-economics the supposition of rational conduct of economic subjects would be misleading, and therefore cannot be admitted. Since all known economic theories are based on this supposition, none of those could be used legitimately in the very small economy. This would leave us empty-handed and saddled with the moral obligation to develop an altogether new approach that does fit the case or take the position that mini-economics is a contradiction in terminis. One might object that multiplicity of roles is no monopoly of very small societies, but a widespread and very common phenomenon throughout humanity. Every subject has its several roles: producer, consumer, child, spouse, elder, member of a conjunction of different groups: family, clan, neighborhood, municipality, county, nation, etcetera. If people caught in the force fields of conflicting roles cannot act rational, this is tantamount to the statement that rationality is not a human mode of conduct at all.

In a way this is what I believe to be true. This means that also in other contexts than mini-economics the supposition of rational human conduct is at odds with the facts and hence not valid. I am not surprised. Years ago I have already expressed my opinion, though on different grounds, that economics as a science could only transcend its primitive stage after dropping the fiction of rational human conduct. However this may be, for the present we are only concerned with decision making within very small systems. For instance, like the two cases in the following narrative.

Once upon a time there were three boys, called Tom, Dick and Harry, who resembled each other so amazingly in looks, conduct and character, that only their respective mothers could tell them apart, at least they thought so. But everybody else took them for identical triplets, especially on Monday mornings in their clean school uniforms. This afforded them no end of mirth, and they became inseparable friends. Those happy years did not last. Their families moved to different cities and they lost sight of one another.

Many years later, in an altogether different place, they met by surprise. Tom had become a doctor, Dick was deacon of the local church and Harry happened to be a diplomat. At the occasion of their quite unexpected meeting they were rather short of time, so they were eager to get together some other time soon. At this point it became at once clear that since the days of yore a number of differences had crept in, associated with their roles in society. They had developed markedly different attitudes toward Wein, Weib und Gesang. Of course they had, all three of them, turned into responsible men of distinction, neither of them given to the coarser forms of boozing, caroling and wenching. But the differences were there all the same.

The doctor regarded alcohol in any form as a threat to physical and mental health. The deacon was wont to write his best sermons in a mellow mood brought on by aged whisky. The diplomat was a veritable expert on vintage wines, with a penchant for red Burgundy.

Also on the fairer sex they did not see eye to eye. The doctor set much store by biological aspects: his ideal woman could be termed a healthy animal. To the deacon women were potential, actual or missed mothers, the heart of home and family life. The diplomat considered presence of the ladies essential to any social or cultural function.

The doctor thought of singing mainly in terms of kitchen sopranos and bath tub baritons: very commendable exercise for the lungs and good for the soul too. No need for tranquilisers there. The deacon associated singing with the choir, euphoniously praising the Lord mainly on Sundays. The diplomat had accumulated an amazing collection of grammophone records and was fully conversant both with grand opera and the romantic repertoire.

Tom proposed to meet one another at a certain day and hour in the local swimming pool, when there would be a bunch of apprentice nurses around, whose clamours and shrieks were music to his ears. For Dick this was much too frivolous. He invited the others for some drinks in the vestry when next to it in the chapel the choir would be rehearsing, because at that time the sexton's wife, a matronly woman, could minister to their comforts, as she had to be around anyway with the key. Harry mentioned a classy restaurant, where both kitchen and cellar were above reproach and where they could be sure of a pleasant evening, with the ladies of course, to a background of refined live music.

Their compromise was predictable. In a quiet hour they met at a convenient club, where the doctor partook of fruit juice as the deacon sniffed the rare fumes of old brandy and the diplomat sipped a very dry amontillado. They had too much to talk about for just one occasion, so they decided to meet again in the same fashion next week. And the next. And so on. Thus they institutionalised the rational compromise of their social interaction, thereby showing themselves to be rational decision makers.

But wait. We will now introduce just one little change, by shifting our focus to a different world, exactly like our own world but for one minor detail. Namely this: Tom and Dick are one person, named Toby-Dick, called Toddy for short by his friends. The deacon is at the same time the doctor. As such, he still has his misgivings about alcoholic beverages, but he is less firm on the subject and has guilt feelings because of his spirituous habits acquired in years of spiritual leadership. In his dealings with females, disparities between the doctor's life and the deacon's lessons nag at his confidence. The deacon is anxious about the religious fervour of the choir's sopranos, because as a doctor he knows too much about psychic effects of hyperventilation. Toddy is not a happy man. He is insecure and tense. Where his two roles clash he is not in accord with himself. But as a conscientious and responsible man he cannot bring himself to take the obvious and easy way out by subordinating one role to the other one.

Upon meeting Harry, who is not in any doubt about his own mind, Toddy is at a loss to state his preferences. So Harry's proposal carries the day, but Toddy feels rather bad about this, as he has not been able to make any contribution to the outcome. Brooding over this for some days, he decides not to be taken in again by Harry's highhanded manners and, if possible, to teach him a lesson. When the day comes, he is definitely not in the mood for a relaxed, pleasant evening with the ladies. The dinner party is a flop and both Harry and Toddy feel that they have made a mistake in trying to revive their childhood friendship. They do not meet again.

Yet in this second case all elements of the first case were present, except for the fact that two roles and their role-specific attitudes were combined in one individual. This one person could not reach the same stable compromise as two people acting one role each, because within himself a stable compromise between the two roles was out of reach. In his interacton with the other party he was unable to express the weighted rationality of both roles, mainly because there seems to be no such thing as the weighted rationality of an internalised role conflict.

An oversimplified figment of fiction, like the above two cases, proves nothing whatever beyond the existence of a vivid imagination on the part of the author. But the ring of its plausibility is so loud that it is worthwhile to verify empirically in how far its implications correspond to reality in very small societies.

From a demographical point of view, the very small economy is also faced with problems foreign to larger systems. Even in absolute numbers rather small migratory movements exert, proportionally, a large influence on the composition of the population and tend to destabilise society. Especially in multi-racial communities there is the added danger of upsetting equilibria between ethnic groups, as their relationships are sensitive to shifts in the proportionality of their numbers. During this century in the Netherlands Antilles there have been fairly strong waves of migration in the wake of economic developments, affecting all six islands. This is not a thing of the past. The lag between immigration and integration is a large one, as, for instance, may be observed in Aruba. Moreover, migration in all its forms is in this part of the world a continuous process that is bound to receive new impulses from economic developments in each and every decade. The necessity to reckon with these effects well in advance adds to the woes of planners in very small economies.

In foreign politics, very small nations are at the lowest end of the scale of power and, moreover, physically not even able to maintain a near complete network of diplomatic relationships, for sheer lack of manpower and funds. Less evident, but nevertheless just as true, they are also very vulnerable in matters of interior politics.

Examples, also recent ones, that a short campaign of one charismatic personality is sufficient to cause a dramatic shift in the balance of power, are abundant. Party allegiances are dominated by particularistic ties and animosities. "Personal antagonisms can poison public affairs while disagreements over policy can estrange private life. There is little room for manoeuvre and, instead of parties based on intellectual convictions or class, factions may spring up which are only kept loosely together by various personal bonds." This statement of Woods[11] aptly depicts the fundamental weaknesses of a too small political field, "... where it is difficult to escape into obscurity or to avoid meeting one's opponents all the time."

Also there is a relative difference in the importance of events, calamities or otherwise, in their impact on society, which tends to increase in a ratio inverse to socio-economic scale. According to Woods there is in very small territories "... a vulnerability to crises and pressures that larger countries can shrug off or overcome."

This brand of political instability is an additional risk factor for private business in very small economies. Notably in the tourist trade political unrest may cause, and has caused, losses to airlines, tour operators and hotel chains, with many unfavourable side effects

11) D.P.J. Woods 'The smaller territories: some political considerations' in: "Problems of Smaller Territories" (ed. B. Benedict), London 1967.

throughout the economy, e.g. in falling levels of employment, increasing balance of paymens deficits, dwindling tax receipts, and decreasing retail business turnovers. In larger countries the action of a small group, for instance ten taxi drivers blocking the entrance hall to an airport, may cause some local unpleasantness, culminating in three or four lines in the evening paper. The same thing on a very small island may cause a chain reaction that is likely to bring the whole economy to a standstill, as the critical mass for fissure is so small. A very small society may be compared to a dry forest in summer, where at all times the temperature is uncomfortably close to the flash point. And though outside observers may by some of the antics strongly be reminded of comic opera, these are more often than not matters of life and death to the participants.

The size of the machinery of government is only partly dependent on the size of the nation, as it has to fit the pattern of constitutional requirements. In very small nations, its elaborate structure may be too heavy a burden for the small tax base. Recruitment of skills, both political and executive, is also problematic, as the number of key positions to be filled is out of proportion to the total size of the community. This situation is generally aggravated, because particularistic party affiliations are a major deciding factor in appointments to government jobs. As Singham[12], discussing the relative scarcity of legislative and executive talent, puts it: "this shortage becomes all the more important in smaller territories where the skills of the 'out' party are not employed."

An other problem, maybe less dependent on the size of a society and more on its level of emancipation, is the tension between new and old elites. Whereas the majority of higher and middle government officials are recruited from the urban higher and middle classes quite a few politicians may come from the lower classes and have rural backgrounds. In many West-Indian societies class differences still parallel colour gradations, which makes it all the worse that there

12) A.W. Singham 'Legislative-executive relations in smaller territories' in: "Problems of Smaller Territories" (ed. B. Benedict), London 1967.

may quite easily be a lack of mutual acceptance between political leaders and their executives. In pointing this out, Singham remarks "If tensions become acute, a pattern of legislative-executive relations evolves that might dramatically be described as one of terror and sabotage."

So, both because of a shortage of proper skills and because of inner tensions, government agencies of a small economy are apt to work less expert and smooth than their counterparts in a larger nation. Here again we find that very small economies operate under less favourable circumstances than larger ones. This is relevant to economic development. Prospective investors in miniature economies may find it near impossible to get the preliminary paper work straightened out within a reasonable time, and may be forced to give up when financial backers lose interest and withdraw from the project. Once a government has acquired an unfavourable reputation in this respect, this will in itself act as a barrier to the entry of new enterprise.

So far in this chapter, a number of aspects has been discussed in which the very small economy differs from larger ones. But they are no more than straws pointing which way the wind blows, as they are not integrated in a conceptual framework that might be regarded as a coherent economic theory of the very small economy. Yet some outlines of such a theory are becoming vaguely discernible.

Whereas most economic theories rest on the interaction of economic forces, we are here faced with situations where these forces are too weak and/or insufficiently integrated to offer a proper explanation of the course of economic developments, a sound basis for forecasts or a suitable handle for policies. Moreover there is the predicament that statistics have a very limited utility because in too many cases the statistical mass is too small for stable aggregates. Economists disregarding these evident facts and blandly proffering macroeconomic models as planning tools for lilliput economies are a disgrace to the profession. I was very disappointed when the Joint Committee of Experts ('Gemengde Commissie van Deskundigen') in their report of July 1979 on the Netherlands Antilles' future[13], disregarded my warnings and took this easy way out of their – admittedly very difficult – assignment.

Economic analysis of very small economies cannot be based on an abstract macro-economic model, but has to take an altogether different approach. It will have to give full weight to all limiting and bordering conditions, whatever their nature, that restrict the free operation of so-called economic forces in a very small economy. Based on this analysis the feasible action spaces of the different branches of economic activity have to be mapped with the corresponding potential outcomes spaces. Also the possible effects of policies on these fields of economic feasibility will have to be assessed. Only after acquiring a thoroughly realistic view of economic possibilities and impossibilities, a consistent set of policy objectives well within the charted spaces, keeping in mind their probable time paths, should be selected. This requires a lot of cooperation between the social sciences and the body political. Above all, it requires an open mind from economists confronted with situations not covered by their text books.

In the case of the Netherlands Antilles there is, at the time this is being written, no indication that the approach advocated here stands any chance to be adopted. I am very pessimistic about the possibility that those responsible for the present collision course will mend their ways in time. The shambles will eventually be blamed on the political leaders of the quarter of a million people concerned and not on outside economic advisers going by the book when they should know better.

13) Gemengde Commissie van Nederlandse en Antilliaanse deskundigen "Aanzet tot een beleidskader", The Hague 1979.

4.

THE DEVELOPMENT ISSUE

The development problem is a multi-dimensional one. A mono-disciplinary approach to it therefore runs the risk of caricaturistic onesidedness. In my opinion, quite a few economists have not steered clear of this danger and it worries me that I may not do much better here. But at least I will try.

The term 'development' carries a positive load. It indicates a complex of processes of change by which in time a new situation in society is reached that is considered to be generally better and more advanced than a previous more backward state. To a fair extent the contents of the term will depend on the values of its user and, of course, one person may welcome progress where somebody else sees his world going to the dogs. But for a start let us stick to the notion that development is essentially a one way process by which human societies wind their way upwards.

In theory there might be, in underdeveloped areas, spontaneous forces at work that if left to themselves would result in development. Something like an invisible hand eventually leading all mankind to bliss. If ever in the past development has anywhere occured in this way, it is certainly not what we observe today in the lesser developed parts of our planet. Wherever development takes place, it is in a context of plans and their implementations. This implies the existence of development policy objectives. One might expect to find what they are pretty soon on acquainting oneself with the subject.

As I had not had previous research assignments in this field, I came to development economics as an outsider, be it one armed with a long and varied experience in sorting out puzzles and problems. Thus I expected to find out quick enough what it was all about. But I struck a major difficulty right there. It was not that I could not find any clear statement of the objectives of development. On the contrary, I came across far too many, at times contradictory, and impressing me as secondary targets derived from some central objective that was not clearly perceived.

The cause of this unsatisfactory state of the art may well be the conspicuous lack of some universally accepted notion of the state or level that is to be reached ultimately by a society through the processes of change that constitute development. Lacking the concept of an ultimate target, different levels of development, both spatially and along the time axis, can only be defined in relation to each other. Developments so defined are no more than relative changes in a drifting field without fixed landmarks. There seems to be a paramount need for a global model describing in non-ambiguous terms the goals of development.

Such a model is feasible. It may be based on the complex of norms covered by the label 'human rights'. This concept has a long history and has finally come of age in our time. It evolved from the growing acceptance of laws protecting the rights of individuals, expanding to more and more aspects of life and well set on a course to balance ultimately the right of every individual with the equal rights of all others. An important day was December 10th 1948, when the "Universal Declaration of Human Rights" was accepted by the United Nations as a common platform. The "European Convention for the Protection of Human Rights and Fundamental Freedoms" (Rome 1950) and the "European Social Charter" (1961) were further developments towards an internationally accepted body of laws aimed at the protection of the natural right of every individual born into this world to have a fair chance not to be frustrated by fellow humans in his attempts to live a truly human life.

If human rights are not honoured to the full, this springs from one (or both) of two causes. First: a society or its leaders may be reluctant to honour these rights, either outright or by giving an interpretation violating their spiritual content. Though this in final analysis concerns us all, it is primarily a problem for the legal professions and for politicians. I will bypass it here. Not so with the second cause: the cases when in a society there simply is no or insufficient scope in the material sense for the full honouring of human rights.

I propose to define underdevelopment in a society as the lack of wherewithal for the full honouring of human rights.

In a society where there are no such shortages or shortcomings everybody could, technically, live as a human should. A society that could, if it wanted to do so, hold out the opportunity for a full human life not to some but to all of its members should not be called underdeveloped. Of course, even in such a society the people may still have many further wishes and ambitions, but the realisation of those should not be termed 'development'. Even though it may not be fair to bundle such further wishes all together and label them 'overdevelopment', we should readily admit that in this direction there is ample scope for more solidarity in the weighing against high priorities elsewhere.

By reserving the term 'development' for changes widening the material scope for the honouring of human rights we can turn this body of laws and norms into a quasi-fixed landmark to show whether development strategies are on or off course. For each and every society in each separate aspect the nature and measure of its need for development in relation to the goal may be unambiguously observed and subsequently be incorporated in an integrated set of development policy objectives, which may then serve as a touchstone for all strategies, tactics and priority rankings.

It is to be expected that this approach will lead to a reassessment of many issues too easily overlooked now in thinking about development, as it is habitually centered on economic issues to the point of obscuring other dimensions. The mode of thinking proposed here would also serve to map pockets of backwardness in rich communities and to limelight areas of overdevelopment. This way a solution of the development problems will no longer be forever drifting away through the preference drifts in a rising tide of incomes and aspirations. On the contrary, we may expect final solutions for the main aspects, even though further developments of the human rights complex will add further touches for a long while to come.

The very use of human rights as a yardstick for development needs will influence the evolution and further codification of those rights. Yet, because in the end the fundamental rights of any individual cannot exceed the equal rights of other individuals and the aggregate rights of all cannot exceed the material possibilities of their implementation, we may expect this target for the ultimate state of human society to approach gradually to a stable equilibrium. For practical purposes within a limited time horizon we may therefore use the target as a fixed point in a multi-dimensional outcomes space. In these terms development will be measurable in a quasi-cardinal system where solutions are solutions. Possibly the most important aspect of this philosophy is that it helps us to get used to think about progress not as a one-way race into infinity, but as that which gets us nearer to a human way of life for all.

Back now from Utopia to the pseudo-reality of underdevelopment as perceived by economists. Many of them appear to regard less developed countries mainly as nations lacking prosperity. If they admit that the problem has other dimensions as well, they are often too ready to assume that such other problems are caused by economic backwardness. They are like doctors who regard undernourishment as the only and ultimate cause of all ills. Their thinking rests on historical materialism, even if it is not of the Marxian variety.

The interrelation of the different dimensions of development problems, however, seldom or never has the simple and one-sided causal structure so beloved by economists of all schools. Very often backwardness in the level and distribution of material welfare is not the cause, but the effect of non-economic forces at work in a society. We find this also at the other end of the spectrum in rich societies. There, as Max Weber pointed out, the ethics of protestantism have been instrumental in reaching high levels of prosperity. This may be taken as evidence that over the whole spectrum of various states of economic development non-economic variables are in a fundamental way far more important than economists are ready to admit. Economic science will stagnate as long as its mainstream adepts stick to their attempts to explain economic phenomena from the dynamics of other economic phenomena within a so-callled 'extra-economic' environment.

Am I exaggerating? If so, I am in very good company. Hutchison[1] cites Professor Clower as follows: "If successful prediction were the sole criterion of a science, economics should long have ceased to exist as a serious intellectual pursuit." I do not go all the way along with Clower. Though admitting that there is some truth in his statement, I am more in agreement with Hutchison's comment ". . . that to improve prediction or forecasting in one way or another, or to prevent prediction deteriorating is, and should be, a main aim of economists and that it is *to some limited extent* a feasible aim." In striving for this aim, though, we have to become more and more aware of the shortcomings of monodisciplinary analysis and we will have to develop methods to surmount these barriers to scientific progress.

For multi-disciplinary cooperation without confusing of tongues and without quibbles on demarcation lines, we need seamless joints with other sciences, notably social sciences. To attain these, we should not shirk even a complete reformulation of economics in a more universal analytic framework. As a first approach I advocate one in which at all times an explicit differentiation is made between social processes and the process spaces in which they are confined, allowing for separate analysis of both categories, with the purpose in mind to use the results as building blocks for integrated holistic theories. Process spaces for economic processes range from the all-encompassing one named Earth to ever smaller breakdowns in subspaces.

The smallest subspace in economics is the one encompassing the individual in his capacity of decision making unit. It may be

1) T.W. Hutchison "Knowledge and Ignorance in Economics", Oxford 1977.

visualised as a n-dimensional space marking the latitude of his possibilities in all directions. In this framework man, the whole man, is the *smallest particle* within the concern of economic science. With regard to this smallest particle it is not an axiom and not even a simplifying assumption, that man within the confine of his possibilities acts in a sterotyped way 'for his own good' or 'rational'. This is wholly a field for other social sciences. But whatever economists as such don't know, they do know that he cannot overstep the boundaries of his action space, and that his action space is a niche in a hierarchy of larger and larger similar spaces, where each lower level is circumscribed by higher level restrictions. This Chinese Box model is a far cry from the 'homo economicus' as the *starting point* of economic analysis. The contrast between the underlined expressions should be enough to make the lopsidedness of contemporary economic science stick out like a sore thumb. Economic theory as it stands today is to a wide extent a body of statements on larger systems inferred from theories about the very smallest possible economic system. Thus basic flaws in armchair reflection have been blown up in their carry-over up the scale. In the alternative framework suggested here the course of scientific progress is in opposite direction, from the largest process space, encompassing all social processes past, present and future, which is our world, to smaller and smaller subsystems, thus systematically reducing the margin of error while approaching the boundaries of knowledge in the field of economics.

True, there are some economists who do not suffer from a monomaniacal view of development problems. A fair example is the well-known book of Lewis[2]. In the works of a number of economists relevant for the remainder of this chapter the focus is, however, strongly on economic problems as such. Other dimensions of the issues at stake are largely bypassed. Partly this is an inevitable consequence of the need to narrow down a subject. An author intending to deal with one particular topic cannot go too far afield without

2) W.A. Lewis "The Theory of Economic Growth", London 1955.

confusing his readers. The review of a number of such partial approaches is bound to give an impression of onesidedness, that I would have preferred to avoid.

In his famous book Rostow[3] equates the initial stage of an underdeveloped economy with the pre-Newtonian traditional society, that is characterised by a ceiling for the production per head. Based on new knowledge and changing attitudes, at first concentrated within minority groups, centers of economic progress with an enclave character come into existence in traditional surroundings. Only after these enclaves have begun to spread and to assume a dominant role in society, one may, in this vision, conclude that the development process, with growth as its most important characteristic, has started. Main features are high savings and investment quotes, and particularly the home reinvestment of a large share of the profits. Also this author regards very high productivity gains in agriculture as an essential condition for a succesful start of development.

It is fairly obvious that this author stresses above all the importance of endogeneous economic processes supposed to have been instrumental historically in a number of countries that nowadays belong to the group of more developed countries. Even in those cases he is not unassailably right. In my own country, the Netherlands, economic development in this sense took place in the second half of the nineteenth century. Indeed Rostow's basic condition of a dramatic productivity growth in agriculture was fulfilled. Only, it was located in the East Indies, where it was realised through forced production of raw commodities for the European markets. In the growth of the Dutch economy extorted development aid has been an important factor, if not the deciding one.

There is little need to go through the other four stages of growth of Rostow's system in order to see that this author equates to a very high degree development to economic development, which is here

3) W.W. Rostow "The Stages of Economic Growth", London 1960.

practically synonymous with growth. I hesitate to say that he and numerous other economists preceding and following him in his lines of thought have not considered any other needs and shortcomings of less developed societies than the economic ones. But I do think that their reflections on the other aspects have been too vague. They have assumed too easily that the attainment of 'self-sustained growth' would be a cure-all.

The bracketed expression above was also coined by Rostow[4]. Its generally accepted meaning is a situation conducive to continuous economic growth, when national savings are adequate to finance the investments required for this growth. Here we see progress pictured as a march into infinity: a developed nation is a nation with a continuously rising average income per head that is well above the poverty level.

Demas[5] points out a number of ambiguities in this mode of thinking and finally remarks: "To judge from these exercises, one would think that the necessary and sufficient condition for the achievement of selfsustained growth is that the marginal savings ratio should exceed the average savings ratio for a period of about ten to twenty-nine years." He is clearly less than happy with the mainly abstract and mechanistic approach that is so abundant in this problem field.

It is rather misleading to speak of 'the' development problem. In every less developed society it has its own specific dimensions and it is highly improbable that a standard solution for all through one consistent policy based on universal criteria could work. Nevertheless the development issue has on a world scale the political status of one global problem. The heterogeneity of many problems lumped together under this label is often suppressed because its recognition could be interpreted as a lack of global solidarity. Of course there is

4) W.W. Rostow 'The take-off into self-sustained growth' in: "Economic Journal", March 1956.
5) W.G. Demas "The Economics of Development in Small Countries", Montreal 1965.

such a lack, and a tremendous one at that, but no one likes to stand accused of it. To speak of one gigantic and as such insoluble problem is a mighty good cover for those unwilling to shoulder the responsibility for a continuous attack on the underlying problems one by one.

This dubious global mode of thought has developed after the Second World War. Van Philips[6], in the Introduction of his thesis, has pointed out the importance in this respect of the East-West controversy and the Cold War. In particular the American point of view in matters of decolonisation and development was, even before 1950, strongly coloured by fear for expansion of the communist sphere of influence. No doubt this pattern of thought, in terms of a global strategy, has set an example for developing countries, as it stimulated thinking along similar lines. Not from congruency of their basic development problems, but from the comparative statical notion that the world is split up between haves and have-nots, sprang the eagerness for political cooperation between developing countries. Inter alia through conferences in Bandung (1955), Belgrade (1961) and Cairo (1962) their solidarity took a shape that became a goal in itself. At the first United Nations Conference on Trade And Development (Geneva 1964) a group of 75 developing countries operated as a voting block, though in many respects their economic interests were dissimilar.

This fashion in thought, focusing the attention on international aspects of development, detracted from the attention for specific national and local problems at the grass roots level. Thinking on a grand world wide scale was conducive to the selection of too ambitious strategies, plans and projects, subsequently falling on their faces through lack of proper foundation in the local and regional economic and social structure. Also this global school of thought fostered a climat in which there was a premium in terms of aid on the copying of development aims from leading industrial societies,

6) P.A.M. van Philips "Public Finance and Less Developed Economy", The Hague 1957.

notably with regard to infrastructure. The need for realistic planning in terms of endogeneous requirements and possibilities in the present and near future was often overlooked. 'Scrap heaps in the jungle' is a well known expression coined in the aftermath of such grand failures.

Of course, donor countries did not blame themselves, at least not on the main issues. The disappointing results of considerable means misspent in wrong directions inhibited their readiness to give further help, unless they could get more grip on the way in which the funds were to be spent. Thus it became easy to stimulate projects with spin-offs for their own economies and to block the projects that might harm their interests or mitigate their influence. The tendency to give overmuch weight to the international aspects persisted. So did its corrolary, too little attention for problems at the lowest level. Failures remained abundant. In the long run, however, a number of apparent successes may prove more harmful than outright failures, as development was started in abortive directions and up blind alleys. It is not difficult at all to identify developing nations that would be crushed under the weight of the recurring costs of their too ample infrastructures if aid funds were no longer forthcoming.

The account given here is very sketchy and incomplete. But it is enough to serve as a broad background, against which it is not at all surprising that there is little evidence of more than superficial harmony in donor/client relationships. There is much distrust, wire-pulling and intimidation. This sorry state of things is aggravated by the expertness of most national political leaders to load their home troubles on foreign scapegoats. Through this escape mechanism incompetence, selfishness and outright corruption are too often afforded a protective covering, allowing backwardness to perpetuate itself. In certain cases development aid may strengthen instead of break the vicious circle of povery and its exploitation.

But change is inexorable. Mounting tensions breed forces aimed at revolutionary change of power. With or without help from outside they may have their day. Their focus is mostly on political and social institutions, at times to the point of a spurious belief that a radical change of institutions could in itself be enough to change basic attitudes at the roots of resistance to innovation. But soon new lords come up against the same set of inhibiting factors at home and abroad that tied the hands of their predecessors. This may result in a drift towards radicalisation and the philosophy that power grabbed by force is in itself legitimation to subject multitudes of common village people to 're-education'.

The 'Basic Needs School' is an offspring from such roots. It is not simply an attempt at simultaneous solution of distribution and growth problems in one single development strategy. That might also – and better at that – be achieved through a refinement of current methods of development planning and project selection. In a joint study of the World Bank and the University of Sussex this has been made quite clear by Chenery[7] and his co-authors. In this context the reduction of income inequalities is not a purpose in itself, but has to be judged for its effects on poverty. Poverty is not just lack of money, but a multi-dimensional pattern of life that is apt to perpetuate itself through circular relationships between its various aspects. Mellor[8] formulated this as follows: "Poor health, short life expectancy, little formal education and numerous children per family are the classic features of poverty. Each is both a cause and an effect of poverty; amelioration of each condition is a potential target for specific programs to reduce poverty."

Even when the one and only target is the combat of famine, a reduction of income inequality may result in worsening the plight of the poor: when the supply of food is inelastic. Redistribution of income will hardly reduce the demand for food by the higher income groups, whereas more money in the hands of the poor causes a leap in demand from their side. The resulting price increases constitute a decrease in real income of the poor that may easily exceed the

7) H. Chenery, M.S. Ahluwa, C.L.G. Bell, J.H. Duloy and R. Jolly "Redistribution with Growth", Oxford 1974.
8) J.W. Mellor "The New Economics of Growth" Ithaca/London 1976.

initial nominal increase in their incomes. This is only one of the mechanisms by which a leveling of the income distribution may lead to a loss of real income by the lowest incomes groups.

Development problems are seldom if ever simple. Typically they are too complex for simple, sure and fast solutions. Growth of real production is a necessary, but by no means a sufficient condition to have acces, directly or through trade, to the real goods and services that are indispensible in the combat of poverty. Plans to realise growth are one of the necessities. But the planning approach to growth is fraught with dangers. Mellor has shown how, in the case of economic planning in India, pessimistic simplifying assumptions underlying the models had so much influence on the allocation of means, that this in itself was sufficient to make these glum views come true, as there was simply no scope for anything but stagnation in sectors suppressed in the models. I concur heartily with Lewis[9] as cited by Mellor: "The principal danger of macro-economic exercises lies in its propensity to dazzle."

One of Mellor's observations with regard to a large economy like India must have a much more crucial significance in very small systems: "By making long term restrictions on resources, the Plans left insufficient means for taking advantage of a sudden opportunity for agricultural growth or for increasing exports." There should not be the slightest doubt that I regard macro-economic scenarios for very small economies as very dangerous indeed if taken as a framework for actual policy making.

Mellor's advice is to focus on forms of growth leading to increases in employment and to avoid, in new planning models, a number of dangerous simplifications. Attention to the bottleneck of capital should not lead to the neglect of other factors, even if they are in seemingly boundless supply, like human labour in India. Side by side with the production planning for capital goods increases in the

9) W.A. Lewis "The Theory of Economic Growth", London 1955.

production of wage goods should be programmed. Moreover, one should abandon too restrictive assumptions on the composition of the consumption basket in making forecasts. Finally, no end of flexibility is a must in export planning, as a more rigid approach leaves insufficient room to benefit from newly emerging possibilities in the field of international trade.

The last point is of overwhelming significance for very small and wide open economies, as their vulnerability for impulses originating in foreign trade is so high, that restrictive elements in planning may be branded as abortive and harmful attempts to control that which is out of reach of the policy makers.

The work of Chenery c.s., already mentioned on page 55, was, like Mellor's book, directed at other types of less developed economies than the ones in and around the Caribbean that had attracted my attention. On pages 93 and 94 of their book a typology of less developed economies is presented, that is based on three criteria: the degree of urbanisation, relative scarcity of land and the degree of land ownership concentration. For each of the three dimensions there is a choice between the positions 'high' and 'low'. Of course a country like the Netherlands Antilles could be put into one of the eight boxes of this system, but that would not be very useful, as at least two other factors are of much greater importance. First: the scale factor. Any comparison with other economies leaving this dimension out of the picture is grossly misleading. Second: the agricultural sector is not only absolutely, but even relatively very small. Again any lumping together with dissimilar other economies on criteria of lesser relevance would only lead to confusion. In the approach of Chenery c.s. the accent is heavily on systems large enough for macro- and sectorplanning and, reading the book, I got a sneaking suspicion that only nations with a fairly large agricultural sector could at all have development needs.

The single most important contribution Chenery and his co-authors made is their finding that distributive aims must be pursued as an integrated part of policies for development and growth. The acceptance of this tenet has as its corrolary the necessity of a complete reorientation of development research. In this respect the authors stress three interrelated themes:

1. More understanding is needed of the characteristics of and the relations between socio-economic groups in different types of developing territories, in order to develop a sound base for integrated analysis of growth and distribution problems.
2. The mechnism of leaks of benefits of development programs to others than members of the target groups must be exposed.
3. Allocation problems in a wide sense, not only within, but also outside the market, must be analysed as such and in their relationship to the distributions of ownership and power.

As to the second point, it does not seem superfluous to mention that the incidence and mechanisms of shifting the burdens of programs are also well worth further analysis, whereas the research of multiplier effects is a logical extension of any research of leaks. Research in this vein will contribute to the combat of poverty, not only by the provision of salient new information, but also through reinforcement of the political determination to change society in more egalitarian directions. Without sufficient determination it will be near impossible to achieve anything at all.

But political determination also has its drawbacks, as may be observed with reference to the 'basic needs' approach. This school of thought merits a positive rating for its focus on the problems at the base of society. But it is a pity that much of its development as a philosophy is coloured by an aprioristic ideology, which is apt to turn work at the basic level for economic aims into a means to further political ends. Its great inspiration is 'the big leap forward' in Mao's China. The importance of 'democracy' at the village level is pivotal. What in fact is meant by this may be inferred from the following statement of Khan[10]: "Above all the full participation of the people will have to be guaranteed by the unhindered institution of democracy at the grass roots." This refers not to western or

10) A.R. Khan "Basic Needs: an Illustrative Excercise in Identification and Quantification, with Reference to Bangladesh", I.L.O.-Paper, Geneva 1976.

westernized communities, but to traditional Bangladesh villages, with their age-old fabric of social and economic inequalities. It amounts to an abrupt and complete change of the social system, which is utterly impossible on a voluntary basis. This amounts to intimidation if not naked force in the manipulation of social control within the small rural society to compel all to 'voluntary' labour. In economic terms it is the severing of the bond between labour and its just wage, which in any other context would be branded as gross exploitation by its present advocates. By this device labour, which otherwise would have remained unutilised, may be mobilised for productive purposes in a situation of poverty and stagnation that might aptly be described by a Malthusian wages funds model. In using this 'free' labour for improvements of the infrastructure, for instance irrigation systems, a development in the direction of more prosperity or less poverty may be initiated.

This is not so new. There is a striking resemblance to many cases in the long history of mankind, when lords and overlords extracted labour from their subjects to build roads, palaces and pyramids. From observation I know that the duty to work without wages for a number of days each year on roads, bridges and irrigation works was still in force in the Dutch East Indies. To have people work free or for a few handfulls of rice 'for their own good' has to be surrounded by very strong guarantees to prevent the change of today's dream into tomorrow's nightmare. Such guarantees can only be provided by a sufficiently strong and egalitarian democratic society. But that is not likely to emerge spontaneously from the uprooting of traditional norms and power structures. It would not be tolerated even if it did, by those consolodating their newly won powers at the national level. From this angle also it is not a bad idea at all to take 'human rights' as the proper frame of reference in development thinking.

In macro-plannning for basic needs a minimum level deemed necessary for all, including the poorest, is postulated for food, clothing, housing, education and health. From these norms national production targets are calculated. So far I have not come across any proper explanation how this macro-planning at the top is linked to the micro-mechanisms of execution at the bottom. This strengthens my suspicion that 'basic needs' is not founded on consistent economic thinking, but is mainly a political strategy. Its usefulness should be judged from this angle and not primarily on criteria for economic efficiency.

Meanwhile it is precisely the lack of inner cohesion in the method that has given some economists the idea that the macro-planning technique of 'basic needs' could be suitable in cases where its techniques of execution on the micro-level would be clearly out of order, fitted as they are to mainly agrarian societies with very low levels of productivity showing high hidden unemployment. In the context of planning for the Netherlands Antilles a quite serious attempt was made to develop a basket of 'basic needs' targets, even though the agrarian sector in these territories is very unimportant and levels of poverty generally associated with 'basic needs' are not present. The acceptance of such targets would have meant that for the Netherlands the problems of decolonisation would have been reduced to the realisation of those targets for a limited period. The problem of viability of national independence for the Netherlands Antilles could then have been given the solution of quite a different problem, namely the short and middle term economic viability of the territory under the implicit conditions of distributive norms of the planners. Moneywise it would probably have been a rather cheap solution for the political problem of decolonisation, and it is possibly there that economics came in. Of course, problems of economic and political viability are intermeshed. But the general vagueness of partial application of the 'basic needs' method outside its normal context veils these interconnections. There is an other political aspect involved as well. To use the method only for macro-planning and not for restructuring society from the bottom up is likely to impress people initially with its progressive label, but will make for an aftermath of discontent by the time its conservative and neo-colonial nature becomes clear.

One more aspect should not be overlooked. Planning exclusively in terms of the five target areas food, clothing, housing, education and health is of a heartwarming simplicity and directness that encourages attempts to take the most direct roads to the goal. However, it is not hard to see that in the oversimplified structure of the plans many classes of consumption and potential sources of income are glossed over. Theoretically the use of only half the method could be combined with the mapping of devious and indirect paths to realisation of the targets, but that would imply a much higher degree of sophistication and subtlety on the part of planners, executives and politicians than I have noticed during my research. Repeatedly I came across an almost natural association of basic needs targets with existing pernicious fallacies in matters of selfsupply and selfsufficiency, that favour new abortive attempts at import substitution. Such a policy can at the very best have meagre results in terms of volume, that are bought by a sacrifice of real income. This is caused by the generally high import requirements of such industries, their very modest local contribution to value added and the high proportion of transfers abroad of incomes thus formed.

In very small territories 'basic needs' appears to be worse than useless. It is not at all a new thought that development planning should be aimed at the reduction of poverty and it is likewise a commonplace that economic growth with increased inequality may worsen the plight of the poorest. But there are other, more promising, ways to increase real income along lines conducive to amelioration of poverty. A rather succeful attempt in this field was made by my compatriot Helmers[11]. He analysed criteria for the evaluation and selection of development projects, as building blocks for development plans and strategies. The degree and pace of development depend ultimately on right selection and execution of individual projects as such. To Helmers, a project covers not just the period in which development funds are spent and possibly recovered, but its whole foreseeable life span. Using cost-benefit analysis one can estimate the expected total net benefits of a project. Since 1958 the World Bank has used this method in project evaluation. Helmers has been closely associated with this work on various levels during

11) F.L.C.H. Helmers "Project Planning and Income Distribution", Boston/The Hague/London 1979 (2nd ed.).

many years. Part One of his thesis is a splendid text book on techniques and backgrounds of project planning. Part Two deals with interpersonal and intertemporal aspects of income distribution and gives methods to evaluate distributional effects of projects, as well as the ways to incorporate this information in the cost benefit analysis. With this method from a set of economically viable projects the ones can be selected that are most beneficial to the lowest income groups.

It is likely that an extension of this method could also be used on sector and macro planning levels, approximating ideas also developed by Chenery c.s., though one should not underestimate the technical difficulties of more than indicative cost benefit accounting on those levels of aggregation. In particular when unreliable statistics and a statistical mass too small for stable aggregates would lead to wide margins of uncertainty. This is the common situation in very small economies.

Though heartily recommending Helmers' book to advanced students and scientists in this field, I also must point out its limited scope. On the theory and techniques of project evaluation virtually nothing has been overlooked. But there is a lot more to be said about its aims and the aims of development planning in general. The hallmark of a developed society is not primarily that the level and distribution of personal real income is adequate (according to what criteria?), but that the economy may be considered able, through mechanisms of endogeneous adaptations, to maintain itself at its proper level of prosperity in a continuously changing world. Development hinges on the achievement of a structural transformation resulting in the creation of strong internal linkages, by which token the system should become amenable to efficient policies aimed at providing all its members with the material basis to live truly human lives.

Demas[12] gives the following description of this process of transformation: "I include seven basic elements in the term 'transformation

12) W.G. Demas "The Economics of Development in Small Countries", Montreal 1965.

of the structure of production'. These are the capacity to transform as determined by political and social processes and attitudes; the unification of the national market for goods and services; the shift of labour as between primary, secondary and tertiary sectors of the economy; the development of an increasing degree of interdependence among domestic industries and activities; changes in the importance and composition of foreign trade; the reduction of dualism in the economy; and the development of appropriate institutions."

This is followed by a detailed explanation of the significance of each of the seven points. From this survey the author concludes that full development along these lines is possible only in fairly large economies with correspondingly numerous populations, that to some extent answer the description of a closed economy. Small open economies meet in his opinion with many restrictions, strongly influencing the directions and scope of development. Even after transformation has been achieved these forces will subject economic life to strong pressures of external factors. We will have a better look at this in the next chapter.

The need for development and development aid is so widespread that we may be tempted to generalisation of the ills and cures of backwardness. But we should remain at all times wide awake to the fact that, in different parts of the world, the present situation has emerged in a very heterogeneous historical and cultural context. Even where parallels and similarities in causes are found there are more often than not major disparities in force and impact from place to place and between different periods.

Universal factors making for differences in development level between societies may be of a given and unchangeable nature. The slant of the Earth's axis relative to its plane of circulation around the Sun, in combination with a given distribution of sea and land areas over our globe, makes for climatological differences generally favouring temperate zones that are not landlocked, and disfavouring many territories between the tropics of Cancer and Capricorn.

Formally we may not be able to exclude the possibility that other universal factors could be derived from the biological and general behavioural heritage of humanity as a natural species. But in the main differences in human conduct and attitudes making for divergences in economic development between various societies are to be seen as characteristics stemming from different cultures and the frictions and clashes between them.

It is an undeniable fact that amongst the different cultures its modern western variety has assumed a leading role. It has also usurped the role of standard in development thinking and we may well have our doubts whether this augurs so well for the future of mankind. It would be a mighty good thing if, in our fervour to promote development of the Third World, we could curb our cultural imperialism and cultivate a proper respect for what is still left of older cultures often encompassing human values we have to learn or maybe relearn. A major step in this direction would be to regard the removal of physical and social constraints on fundamental human rights as the touchstone for progress. Not prosperity in the customary materialistic sense is the goal, but a full and rewarding life for the many, in terms of their own social and cultural values. Up to a point, the rise of real income has its utility as a means to this end. Not far beyond this point it detracts from the goal through its contribution to mundial inequality.

This, in plain words, means that the benefits of any policy, program or project should not only be spelled out in terms of the income and distributional effects on the target groups, but also in terms of their effects on the donors and the executors of the plans. These evaluations should not be restricted to 'economic' dimensions, but be made to include explicit forecasts of the short and long term effects on the development of the scope for at least the most fundamental aspects of human rights.

5.

A BIRD'S EYE VIEW OF THE FIELD

So far the field of mini-economics is largely uncharted and lacks proper theories. The purpose of this chapter is therefore twofold:

a. to compile a first collection of possible topics for future research and
b. look around for possible building blocks for mini-economic theories.

The first part of this assignment was approached in a fairly systematic way. I prepared three preliminary lists. The first one consisted of all instances I had collected of possible influences of scale restrictions. The second listed aspects of underdevelopment. The third contained seven elements of the development process as listed by Demas, extended with an eighth point referring to human rights. Cross tables of these lists were my guide lines in writing the text. Though I cannot guarantee completeness, there seems to be a fair chance that no important links between scale restrictions and development problems are overlooked. The focus on these links is at the cost of a certain onesidedness. This becomes clear as soon as we take a look at the second purpose of this chapter.

Small scale is, as I see it, not an economic variable in its own right, but a context in which the dynamics of a society are influenced by a number of bordering conditions, that range from very hard to soft. They encompass at least three categories: they may have a. technical, b. institutional and/or c. psycho-social features. In so far as they are rooted in scale restrictions, and an increase of scale is not feasible, their nature is permanent and structural. As such they have exerted influence on development in the past, continue to do so in the present and may be considered significant to the development process in the future.

At this point however we must be aware of an other major aspect: ISOLATION. There was a time when very small societies were the rule rather than the exception in our world: when transportation and communication were too primitive to support the reach of a system of domination over domains too large to be crossed by foot within a few days. With the development of transportation and communication ever larger systems became feasible and evolved. Small societies persisted mainly by virtue of an isolated position. As isolation of societies is conducive to non-parallel development, the result is not only the existence of development arrears in most very small states, but also cultural, social and economic heterogeneity in the group of small nations, even to the point of superficially rendering absurd my contention that as a group they have enough in common to merit serious scientific attention.

Summing up: a mini-economic theory should encompass in one way or another two triangles:

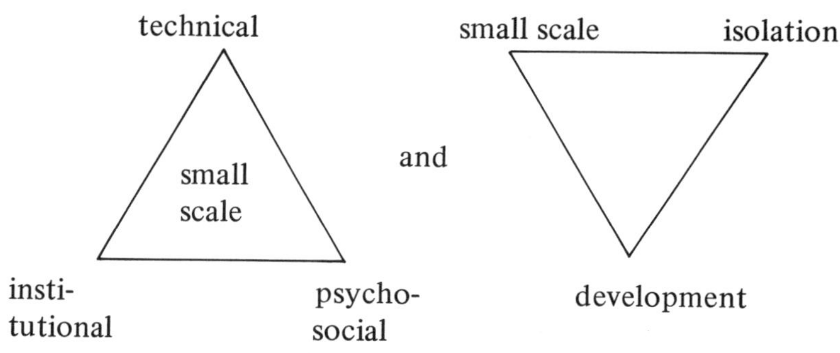

It must be clear that a search for links between scale and development is directed at only one side of the second triangle. Even so, the checklist presented in the remainder of this chapter is fairly long.

A major cause for economic backwardness is contained in the climatological givens, like sunshine, rain, drought and extremes of heat or cold. They are the inexorable forces of nature. Life, in particular human life, has to adapt to them or perish. If a country is large, there is a fair chance that in different parts it will have a scala of different climatological conditions, widening the range of primary production possibilities for its national market. A very small country lacks this diversity and is probably limited to a rather small number of crops. Adverse weather conditions causing only local crop damage in large countries may wipe out the whole harvest when the whole country is hit by the same storm, drought or whatever it is.

The relative impact of a calamity, say a flood or an earthquake, is inversely proportional to the size of the society. Even if all land areas on our globe were equally prone to disasters, which they are not, the very small countries would be harder put than larger ones to overcome such setbacks. The same goes for epidemics and wars.

In many places man, by his disastrous impact on ecological surroundings, has so increased the threats to his own survival, that the extra slice of bread, that could have been foregone for investment in a brighter future, simply was not available. Here again, in a larger nation development in some regions favoured by initially better conditions, could provide both the source and the impetus for programs of flood and erosion control, irrigation schemes etcetera, eventually overcoming the barriers to progress in the blighted area. On the other hand, if in past years of ignorance a very small country has been stripped of its original protective vegetation, and subsequently has lost most of its precious topsoil, there is within its borders not even enough virgin land left to make a fresh start. Its population is doomed to eke out a living somehow in an environment offering no scope for endogeneous progress.

To the natural and man made causes of backwardness, land ownership and use may be added as a staunch third. In larger countries inequalities in land tenure have tended to induce migration from rural to urban regions, thus providing the labour force for industry. In very small countries there is virtually no place to go where chances might be better. Emigration is the only alternative. As emigrants are typically the more alert, energetic and healthy members of the community, society is drained of the forces that might have contributed to reforms.

Inequalities in land ownership are generally part and parcel of a vast complex of social and economic inequalities. To safeguard and retain their privileged positions, a traditional élite will oppose progress when it threatens the status quo. Land ownership offers them a good grip, particularly in a small society with few if any outsiders. Particularistic relationships lead to systems of patronage, continually reinforcing social immobility. Restrictions of scale increase the rigidity of social structures and are a brake on progress that is absent in larger systems.

More affluent members of very small societies find only limited opportunities for productive investment of their savings at home. But it may be significant also that productive investments at home are likely to alter the status quo, which is bound to evoke criticism from one's peers. In a setting of particularistic social relationships this is a serious matter. Even avowed protagonists of economic progress may be found to prefer saving abroad to the prospect of sticking their necks out at home. Known cases where the words of prominent members of small societies are at variance with their acts may be more satisfactorily explained by this mechanism than by the assumption of a negative correlation between personal status and personal morals. However this may be, savings leaking abroad are a drain on economic development.

Traditional patterns of social immobility may in turn aggravate the drawbacks of a very small social field. To the stress induced by multiplicity of roles is added the intergenerational stress caused by the handing down of norms and values less and less natural to younger generations that are increasingly affected by the mundial information explosion. This increases the chances of an eventual uprooting of the traditional social system, which in itself will not solve development problems and may complicate matters through discontinuities in economic life and development aid.

The tensions of accumulated social stress in a very small society are a good breeding ground for political careers of 'reformers', whose main attraction is quite often their personal charisma. They constitute a perennial threat to the establishment, which is thereby motivated to entrenchment of its positions of power and authority.

Rule by a 'strong man', determined to uphold traditional views, even with the trappings of parliamentary democracy, is likely to be at the same time an obstacle to reforms and a natural target for the forces of discontent. Especially the latter may prove harmful: when the opposition forces get the upper hand it may soon become clear that they had only a common enemy and no common goal beyond. In the ensuing confusion the old order is likely to be restored, be it with some new faces in key positions. In a highly charged political field that is too small for clear distinctions between personal and social aims a reformer must have exceptional qualities indeed to achieve anything worth while.

There is yet an other way in which a traditional pattern of relationships, that is often characteristic for underdevelopment, may interact with scale restrictions. In very small countries the number of political and administrative key positions is not really that much smaller than in larger societies, bound up as it is with constitutional and bureaucratic requirements. The ensuing recruitment problem is quite often aggravated through emigration of talented youngsters and by political factionalism excluding members of opposition parties. If on top of this traditional norms narrow down the choice to members of élite groups, chances are that many positions will be held by individuals deficient in the proper qualifications for their tasks. Backlogs of development tend to remain preserved in very small societies traditionally underutilising the talents of many of their members.

A low average income per head, often in combination with glaring distributional inequalities, is both a clear sign and a cause of backwardness. To raise the average income per head, total annual production has to grow at a higher rate than population. The reduction of inequality by redistribution through taxation is even in developed countries a rather inefficient tool. In developing countries such policies would be futile if they stopped short of fundamentally changing the social order. If that is the aim, well and good, but then it makes little sense to make this detour. If the aim is evolution to less poverty a better way than redistribution is improvement in the structure and composition of production along lines that make a significant part of the benefits accrue to the lower income classes. As mentioned in the previous chapter there are sound methods to select projects that contribute to the combat of poverty through viable economic development. A prerequisite for this method, however, is the existence of the proper alternatives to choose from. This precondition is often not fulfilled in the very small economy. Its endowment with natural resources is likely to be narrow, excluding many production possibilities right from the start. An other bottleneck may be the absence of trained workers and the impossibility to set up technical schools for too small numbers of students.

Not only lack of materials and qualified workers, but also scarcity of good locations may in very small economies block otherwise feasible projects. If to overcome such handicaps governments offer tax incentives to prospective foreign investors, this means that the benefits of projects are allowed to leak abroad to a larger extent than in the case when there are no disadvantages to be offset.

If a project entails the home production of goods that were formerly imported, the importers stand to lose. In large economies their chances to block or even hinder the project will be negligible. In very small systems their relative importance is so much greater that they may cause a lot of trouble. If the start of, say, a soap factory is not accompanied by an import ban on soap, the venture is likely to be pushed into the red by dumping practices. In such a case, when an import stop was announced, before it came into effect the importers, backed by credit from foreign producers, built up stocks for several years and quietly got ready for all obstruction and wirepulling they could muster. In the particularistic setting of a very small society there is ample scope for this.

In a previous chapter mention was made of the fact that a very high proportion of imported goods in a very small economy consists of consumer items, with significant risks of pilfering at the ports of entry. Here also is a nexus with poverty, but it may be a weak one. If the spoils were only consumed by the poor, this might be seen as an informal redistribution of income, that could be dubbed the Robin Hood effect, with more affluent consumers through higher prices subsidising their less fortunate fellows. But chances are that the distribution of spoils is much less equitable and that a sizeable part of the burden is borne by the lower income groups through the prices of the necessities of life. In several Caribbean islands I have met traders estimating the damage through pilfering and shoplifting at well over ten percent of the c.i.f. value of total imports. Information from other sources (shipchandlers, insurance brokers, port authorities) tended to support these estimates.

Societies ridden by poverty and inequality have high instability risks, which in the very small economy are aggravated because the effect of a given event tends to be inversely correlated with the size of the system affected by it. They may therefore easily miss opportunities through too unfavourable risk assessment by potential foreign investors.

With this collection of observations the links between poverty and small socio-economic scale have by no means been explored to the full, but that is an impossibility in the context of one chapter in one small book.

Lack of adequate development may hinge on the techniques and organization of production. Inefficient small scale manufactures in a very small nation are much easier replaced by foreign mass goods than upgraded by improved processes and methods. Even more so if better techniques are only efficient at production levels exceeding demand in the home market. Better organization and division of labour may run up against the same snag.

In a very small economy the exports are often limited to a small number of commodities. Raw materials or intermediate goods, like phosphate, copra, livestock, salt and sugar. It would be advantageous to export the goods in a more finished or less raw state, to increase national income through higher export revenues. Again, in a very small economy this may be impossible, not only because of the risks attached to new enterprise lacking the firm base of an adequate home market, but even because the total quantities of production may be insufficient for proper use of the techniques. It is hard to imagine that the right location for a fish cannery could be a place where henceforth fish would have to be imported to allow the factory to run at an acceptable level of utilisation of its capacity.

One of the dimensions of backwardness may be population pressure, meaning that the productivity of an area is inadequate for its inhabitants. Large parts of the Third World are faced with this problem and it is not surprising that small societies share in this fate. Even so, there are interactions between this aspect of underdevelopment and the restrictions of small scale that we should not allow to be blotted out under the immensity of the global problem. The typically very limited set of natural resources in a very small economy is an overall restriction on its spectrum of production possibilities. Faced with too many impossibilities, the very small society is likely to run out of answers to the demands of an increasing population long before this at the same population density would happen in less onesidedly endowed larger systems.

The above formulation is in comparative static terms, but that should not be read as a negation of the truly dynamic nature of these problems. The boundaries for the viability of a human system are never completely fixed, but subject to changes both through exogeneous events and through interactions between the system and its environment. The latter forces have in many instances an overall negative trend through ecological damage, but the surprising fact is that traditional methods of conservation in a number of very small societies, notably in the Pacific, have been effective in preventing the exhaustion of resources. Those societies seem to be traditionally in step with attitudes that should be universal if we accept the 'Gaia hypothesis'[1] or, less far reaching, the common sense thesis that for long term survival of mankind humanity should be a partner in the total system of terrestrial life and not its myopic exploiter. At least we should explicitly be aware of the fact that the carrying capacity of an area is a function of the way it is exploited, and that the effects

1) J. Lovelock "Gaia: a New Look at Life on Earth", London/New York 1979.

of this exploitation are not confined to one particular area, but may have repercussions elsewhere and possibly everywhere.

From times immemorial migration has been an answer to population pressure. In a very small nation migration from rural to urban areas is rather futile, as total distances are so small that the move brings the migrant not significantly nearer to new opportunities beyond the old horizon. So only emigration offers new opportunities, and this solution is often sought. Emigrants are overwhelmingly the more active, healthy and enterprising members of the society. Their depart may effect local production more than consumption and thus not result in larger shares for those remaining. The emigration of its ablebodied fishermen has deprived in some known cases the community, with its disproportionate numbers of young, old and infirm, from the protein base of its subsistence diet. If the emigrants send enough of their earnings home to their relatives, this spending power may allow them to live on imports replacing former domestic production. Several small island economies in the Caribbean are at times labeled as paycheck economies. They show anomalies like distinctly separate price levels for cash and account sales, and the concomitants of boredom in places where the possibilities for consumptive activities are restricted and both the need and the scope for work to generate income are small. I, for one, am not at all envious of those who have the time to play dominoes all day long in the shade of a tree. Not just one day, but every day.

Malnutrition and poor health go side by side with poverty and are deterrents of progress in their own right. They are by no means particular to very small nations, though the chances of an ill balanced diet may be somewhat larger in a small territory with restricted production possibilities than in countries large enough for more varied food production. As to health care the general standards are not lower in small countries than elsewhere, but there are bottlenecks. Health care in very small societies cannot cater to relatively rare diseases needing specialists and facilities that only in much larger systems would be regularly needed. The absolutely small turnover of drugs and other medical supplies causes problems in stockkeeping of items that cannot be kept too long without losing quality. Even minimum stock requirements for goods of high durability which are rarely needed may constitute such a deadweight on the budget of a very small country, that it leads to a lowering of standards and taking unwarranted chances. Compared to population size the number of doctors may look ample, but because of their absolute small numbers discontinuities are quite common, through problems with replacement during absence or illness.

Lack of adequate education is both a cause and a hallmark of backwardness. In larger territories one of its aspects may be lack of social and geographic mobility of many potential students, depriving them from the benefits of facilities that, somehow, are available. In very small societies many forms of education are completely absent, because of too small numbers of potential students for financially viable organization of their tuition. Even at the secondary level there is often not much differentiation in types of schools.

The more affluent families tend to send their sons to schools abroad and there may even be provisions for the sponsoring of bright youngsters of more humble origins. But particularly if they are intelligent, education abroad is bound to make them aware of the many restrictions of life at home and at the same time forces them to become adapted to life amongst strangers. Many will not return at all or, if they do, will leave again when they become dissatisfied with the limited scope for careers in the familiar setting. Education abroad is a drain on the talents of a very small society.

Those of the younger generations who are less lucky and have to make shift with the limited possibilities of local formal education, are at the same time increasingly exposed to informal education by television, radio, press and movies. This may make for a wide rift between their aspiration levels and the very modest scope for attainment. It would be too simple to say that lack of good educational facilities in very small countries is the main cause of alienation, but it certainly is a contributing factor.

In a very small society the nexus between higher education and emigration may even be discernible in a demographic sense. The balance between higher status boys and eligible local girls will be upset if many of the former marry abroad. The less lucky of the latter group may miss out on marriage altogether if they don't settle for partners of lower status. If in the lower status groups there is also a shortage through emigration of young men of marrying age, the bottleneck is pushed down the scale and there is a great likelihood of downright poor marriage prospects for young women of the lowest income and status groups. My rather incomplete observations point in this direction in 'paycheck economies', but much more evidence over a wider range is needed for firm conclusions.

Great inequalities in the distribution of power are a further common trait of many backward societies. The tools of power are by no means limited to threats with, and use of brutal force, but include social and religious traditions, manipulation and blackmail. The wielding of naked force is not a sign of strength, but rather the expression of feelings of insecurity by those in power. More secure systems of dominance rely on their more subtle tools. Thus rules and regulations in a very small society are easily turned into tools of dominance. For instance, the granting of tax and other incentives to investors does not have to be an automatism, but may be a mechanism conferring power on the men at the top. Likewise, the offer or withdrawal of protection in the home market has its uses as a reward or a punishment, obviously to the detriment of economic development.

By no means all incumbents of power in miniature states are content with the roles of inconspicuous Macchiavellis. A hunger for outward signs of status, even when falling short of megalomania, may divert already tight funds into uses for prestige projects, crowding out more beneficial uses of the funds. Foreign exchange spent on exclusive cars and expensive foreign building materials is a dead loss for the combat of poverty.

In very small societies patronage is often the fabric of its power system. It is fuelled by the diversion of funds to unproductive uses. Yet such systems may be unstable.

To those not in power the inequalities of the system are additional risks when it comes to the investment of their savings, making them very reluctant to sponsor ventures in their home countries. At the same time those in power may not feel any too secure either or may deem the present the proper time to take out insurance for future uncertainties: their savings will also leak abroad.

One might be tempted to think that the presence of a strong dominance system in a very small social field may have its advantages if the power is used in a beneficial way. For instance, in the institution of measures of hygiene and the introduction of new production modes. As a logical possibility this cannot be excluded, but the record of power in the name of progress is poor. Its monuments are like cathedrals large enough to seat the remaining population five times over in faraway places bypassed by prosperity and progress.

In the personalistic setting of a very small society a system of dominance depends on the personal power of its leader and hence is unstable. Lack of stability in a power system increases its drawbacks and diminishes its possible advantages. It is hardly to be expected that in such circumstances centralistic rule, implementing successive five year plans, would be a fitting strategy for development. But development without proper plans or their right execution looks just as impossible, and there may be only a razor's edge between the two extremes.

Lack of development funds is a first class reason for lack of development. Very small nations are nowhere when it comes to that, unless they are lucky enough to come under agreements with their former colonial overlords. Even so the bureaucratic trappings of such agreements, especially if they are drawn up for larger nations, are veritable beds of Procrustes, on which the very small are mercilessly stretched beyond their possibilities. In multilateral development the very small tend to be crowded away from the nipples of the international sow by their bigger brothers and sisters in misery.

In getting development funds for infrastructure the handicap of being small shows itself quite clearly. Small projects, in line with the requirements of a very small economy, are generally considered too unimportant by outside decision makers. So to get any aid at all one has to come up with plans for airports, roads and ports that would look modest in other places, but really are outsize for the country that, when all is said and done, will be saddled with their exploitation and maintenance. In the Netherlands Antilles, for instance, there are four international airports on six small islands. In Curacao a spectacular high four-lane bridge spanning Anna Bay offers a splendid sight, reminiscent of Sydney Harbour, but it was not really needed to get from one end of the island to the other. The impressive network of speedways in this island, with the latest in traffic lights and some crossings too wide for those pedestrians unable to run for it, does also seem to be out of harmony with reasonable transportational needs of less than 175,000 people on an island of about 180 square miles. But by virtue of this infrastructure the motor car density per mile of road now surpasses that in large metropolitan areas, which in turn made it necessary to institute a well-equipped traffic police force. Needless to say that these largely consumptive developments constitute such a drain on the resources of a very small country, that they are a threat to further progress and to financial viability of true independence. The minimal financial requirement for being one's own boss is a structural balance between running domestic income and running expenses. Outsize infrastructural presents may easily disturb such a balance or the chances of ever attaining it in a very small economy.

An aspect of underdevelopment that constitutes one of the largest problems in the Third World is pauperism. Here at last the very small economy appears to have the advantage. Total distances being small, the move from rural to urban environment is much less alienating in a very small society than in a large country. The social fabric remains intact and though there may be poverty, it is at least shared with one's kin. There is dualism all right in the very small backward economy, but the proceeds of informal urban markets tend to spread to rural areas, as in turn the produce of subsistence agriculture is shared with clan members in town. Although this tends to lessen extreme inequalities in poverty, it would not be right to overlook the problems of pauperism and dualism in the very small economy, on account of idyllic notions on the elasticity of its social ties.

Some remarks are necessary on the subject of physical constraints on human rights. Though the formal adherence to codes of human rights may be largely a political and legal matter, the extent to which any right may be honoured also depends on the physical possibility to do so. Freedom of press presupposes the economic viability of a free press. Equal rights for men and women remain empty phrases if their respective opportunities are grossly unequal and the means to change this situation are simply not available. If we agree that the honouring of any right has its physical requirements, this is tantamount to the thesis that any particular bundle of human rights needs for its honouring an adequate level of livability. In this sense underdevelopment is a constraint on human rights. Also, the ultimate goal of development coincides with the purpose of human rights, that every human being should have the opportunity to live a truly human life. The codifications of human rights are at present in a state of underdevelopment, but we may confidently expect that in their development they will converge towards the equilibrium of the rights of the individual with the equal rights of all other individuals.

To specify the required level of livability for this point of equilibrium thus would be equivalent to the specification of a final goal for economic development.

Further development is not required to allow people to live good full lives and may be formally termed overdevelopment. Resources spent in this direction contain elements of waste in the face of backwardness still depriving far too great numbers of fellow humans of an adequate material basis for the effectuation of their basic human rights.

This issue transcends all differences between large and small societies. Only through research can we establish whether scale factors in very small societies are in fact additional constraints on their livability levels, and thus on their effective scope for the honouring of human rights. But seeing, so far in this chapter, that there are indeed many instances of probably strong links between barriers to development and restrictions of socio-economic scale, it is to be expected that unequivocal clear description of all aspects of the livability levels in very small societies will be crucial, not only to a joint study of their problems, but also to the promotion of joint efforts toward their alleviation or, if possible, elimination. For this reason the description of the livability indicators of very small societies, in a consistent way allowing direct comparisons, should have top priority in any research program aimed at the group of very smalll countries or one of its subgroups.

Having reviewed a fair number of causes and concomitants of underdevelopment in their possible relationships to aspects of scale in very small societies, we will try to do the same with different aspects of development processes. In this we will by and large be guided by Demas[2]. He puts "the capacity to transform economic life in the perspective of political and social attitudes" in the first place, and rightly so. This means that we have to attach great importance to the aspects in which these attitudes in very small societies tend to differ systematically from what might be expected in larger systems. In this respect the single most important factor is also the main characteristic of a restricted social field: particularism as a perennial obstacle to universalistic economic decision making. It is underlying numerous situations detrimental to the transformation processes.

In a personalistic setting it is very difficult to bridge long standing antagonisms and feuds for the sake of progress. Even if at some moment a truce between factions is negotiated, chances are that it will not last long, as even the best universalistic policies for progress will be judged in a personalistic light. Not only by those actually hurt, but also by people doing quite well, but jealous of others presumably doing better yet right under their noses. Humans are humans, not saints.

Connected with this is the general atmosphere of tension, bred by the stress of multiple roles, to which many if not all decision makers are subjected. That atmosphere is not conducive to efficient imple-

2) W.G. Demas, "The Economics of Development in Small Countries", Montreal 1965, p. 150.

mentation of plans, because of interfering emotional side issues. It even becomes difficult at times to see what are the main and what are the minor problems. At first I was amazed when I observed repeatedly that persons of high responsibility appeared to be quite unable to delegate very minor decisions to their staff and thus allowed themselves to become snowed under in trifles. It took me quite some time to understand the nature of this phenomenon and longer yet to realise that I, coming from a much larger social system, might not be a good judge on the relative importance of apparently small matters. However this may be, the impossibility to reduce policy making to actions on main issues only is an obstacle to attempts at transformation of the economy.

An other problem is lack of clarity in political objectives, which may be encountered in systems where political parties are less formed around principles and programs, and more around personal leadership resting on power or charisma. Government decisions on economic issues cannot be taken just for their expected effect on long term development, but have to take into account the expectations of their immediate influence on local politics. Along this way economic progress may be very hard to achieve, but any other strategy that makes one lose the next election may be less efficient yet.

Social and economic attitudes towards development may be severely biased by the structure of land ownership. In a small country the total amount of economically useful land is restricted. The ownership of plots by people unwilling to sell may create serious bottlenecks, by blocking infrastructural developments, or through unavailability of good building sites for industry and housing.

We must also keep in mind that investment in real estate is traditionally regarded as the safest investment in the home country. A land owner may refuse to sell if there is no other land available to be bought at reasonable terms with the proceeds of the sale. Moreover, if he does not need the cash, he may expect a rise in the scarcity value of his property exceeding normal interest rates. In many places land reforms and even nationalizations may be necessary preconditions to economic progress.

In social and economic attitudes inhibiting progress, we must not overlook the nexus between development and emancipation. Old and new élites alike may feel threatened by formerly discounted social groups demanding recognition of their rights. Personalistic overtones of the ensuing conflicts may in a small society lead to entrenchment of the establishment along conservative lines. If the very small economy is to advance, its leaders must have a lot more tolerance and wisdom than is generally required in larger systems.

The second element of the development process, in Demas' vision, is the development of an integrated national market for goods and services. This means in the first place that barriers to domestic communication and transportation should be removed to such an extent that, in a territorial sense, there are no isolated areas left that cannot effectively participate in economic life and are subject to discrimination. But 'integrated market' means also integration between different sectors of the economy, which is necessary for the creation of a network of linkages that is indispensable as the mechanism through which beneficial impulses in some sectors can spread to other sectors, instead of leaking away abroad. Progress is bound to be very slow if development projects do not have significant spin-offs within the economy. Without these take-off into selfsustained growth must be considered impossible.

In the very small open economy we cannot overlook the utter impossibility of anything beyond a rather incomplete and fragmentary production structure, and an inevitably large import leak of the multiplier. Investment goods are imports, as well as large proportions of raw materials, intermediate goods and wage goods. The scope for a national market for intermediate goods and services is exceedingly small and hence in such an economy linkages between producers are largely absent. Therefore the creation of an integrated national market in a very small economy is only to a small extent possible and will not result in an allocation mechanism that may be trusted with the role of an 'invisible hand' regulating economic life.

A well developed national market for final goods and services is all that is possible and it will have to serve. Even with a huge import leak total consumption will influence domestic production of goods and services. This is not an unmixed blessing when the marginal propensity to consume imports is greater than the marginal propensity to consume. In that, fairly common, case raising prosperity threatens the balance of payments. This leaves the government of a miniature state very little leeway to pursue growth policies. Restrictions on the import of consumption goods may become a dire necessity, though it may be difficult to institute them in the face of powerful neighbors, and even so will lead to the trouble and costs of enforcement.

Lacking a proper allocation mechanism, the very small economy is unable to regulate itself along time-hallowed liberal lines. The choice for a government in this fix might look to be that between central planning and ad hoc stopgap measures if and when the need arises. But full fledged central planning presupposes a strong centralistic government and a bureaucracy ample enough to monitor the economy and include an extensive production planning department. This top-heavy setup is beyond the possibilities of a very small society. It will not last long, unless it is virtually taken over by politically interested outsiders.

This leaves the ad hoc variety as indeed the most frequent type of economic 'policy' encountered in reality. Malta is a possible exception, as far as I could make out from its planning documents. It has a rather flexible indicative planning for a number of years ahead that looks commendable and may work to a certain extent. Again, it may not. Very small societies simply cannot afford to pursue policies all their own, disregarding the many events over which they have no control. That hard fact of life is also a good reason to doubt the feasibility of central planning in the very small economy.

It will be far from easy to develop a workable solution to the needs of consistent policy making in a situation where 'laissez faire' is equivalent to no policy at all. Depending on the case, there may be possibilities to insulate part of the economy against too frequent exogeneous shocks and at the same time seal it off from ad hoc domestic policy changs. A managed enterprise zone might be the right tool for this purpose. Its description can be found in Chapter 5 of "A Road to Full Employment"[3].

The third element in transformation of the economy is a shift of production and labour from primary to secondary and tertiary production. Shifts of labour from primary production will inflate the informal sector to the extent that secondary and tertiary sectors fail to absorb them and opportunities for emigration are lacking. The shift between sectors requires a dynamic balance that may be postulated in models and demonstrated in simulations, but seldom if ever attained in reality. 'Economists simulate it with models' may be a funny slogan, but it does little to cover up the essentially messy nature of processes of change upsetting the lives of people of flesh and blood caught between the ambitions of too optimistic planners and the realities of a small and inflexible economic system.

The very small economy, with its fragmentary production structure and so many imported consumer goods, that could technically be home produced, may appear to an outsider as having plenty of possibilities to extend its production basket of goods and services. As was argued in a previous chapter this view is erroneous. For many goods the minimal production volume compatible with economic feasibility will exceed demand in the home market, while realistic prospects for profitable export of the surplus are nonexistent. If the production scale does fit the domestic market, consumers may yet, for reasons of cost, quality or taste, or even for no apparent reason at all, adhere to their long standing preference for the imported good. The remedy for that not uncommon case is a ban on imports, creating a new black market and a formal monopoly in one masterful stroke, that does very little to insure the efficiency and competitiveness of infant industries. It tends to lead to welfare losses of consumers who, through inflated prices, are forced to subsidise not

3) A.J. Butter "A Road to Full Employment", Amsterdam 1983, ISBN 90 6032 239 8.

only a number of marginal job opportunities, but marginal employers as well.

In a dynamic context things look worse yet. The very small economy cannot possibly be any way near autarchic, unless it be on a very low pre-modern level. So it has a structural need to earn enough foreign exchange to pay for its necessary imports. Therefore a significant part of its productive potential must be earmarked for this purpose. If too much labour and capital is absorbed by government services and production for the home market only, the remaining potential for exports becomes too small. The society becomes economically unviable and will need permanent aid.

In a very small economy the market for exports is, geographically, near its maximal size, whereas the home market is very restricted. Technological advances associated with increases in the optimal volume of production can at least in theory always be accomodated in export industries, but are generally out of reach of import substituting industries. This increases the probability that the latter industries will, within a relatively short time, turn from assets to the economy into liabilities. Even without technological arrears this may also come about through a rising wage level. Expansion to absorb rising wage costs is in a very small market physically impossible.

The absorption of labour in industries and services will tend to be slow, yet erratic. It will demand more than a fair share of care and inventivity in the face of repeated disappointments, all the time only a razor's edge away from imbalances to the other side. A factory employing one thousand men is not large by any standard. But to set it up in a very small economy will create tensions in its restricted labour market and may even induce an immigration wave. Even on a smaller scale this happens whenever new techniques require abilities not or insufficiently available in the work force.

In the discussion of point two, the development of an integrated national market for goods and services, the major problem of a too narrow base for linkages within the national production structure was already mentioned. Demas lists the need for the creation and strengthening of linkages between domestic industries and activities as the fourth element that is required in the transformation of the economy. But there is simply no way for the very small open economy to achieve this to a significant extent. Does this mean that economic development in the fundamental sense of transformation of the economy is out of its reach forever?

Depending on circumstances, there may be different answers to this question. A small economy may be or become well integrated in a supranational regional economy. In that case its economic position would be comparable to that of a region in a large national economy. Its road to development may be difficult, but it certainly would not be blocked in principle.

Also, a very small state dwarfed by its nearest neighbour may integrate its economy almost completely with that of its 'protector' and also in this case there is no reason to suppose that lack of domestic linkages would be fatal.

In other cases, when very small open economies do not have such outside supports, there is a very real problem. An economy of that type might yet find, somehow, working substitutes for its lack of inner economic cohesion. In theory at least social cohesion could take its place, if it is strong enough. Maybe there is sense in policies to strengthen social cohesion where policies to strengthen the allocation mechanism are futile.

In ethnically heterogeneous societies this could easily be a matter of several generations, requiring an extraordinary amount of patience and perseverance. It is a rather grim practical joke of creation that mankind has been equipped with a number of in themselves meaningless but plainly visible physical differences, that for ages have fed xenophobia and misplaced feelings of superiority. Maybe it is wrong to attempt selfconsciously to suppress the evidence of our eyes, for fear of being mistaken for racists, and should we explicitly recognise these differences as setting us the task to come of age, and appreciate in them a marvellous scope for pluriformity, enlarging our human possibilities to be uniquely ourselves, different from one another, but all of equal value.

The fifth element in transforming an economy has to do with changes in the composition of foreign trade and in its volume relative to national income. This is a concomitant of changes in the structure of production. Increased home production of finished consumption goods will not only substitute for former imports, but will also influence the import of capital goods, raw materials and intermediate products. In a restricted home market the accent in industries catering to it may well be on the final stages of production in lines where this is compatible with the scale of efficient production techniques. Between them the import costs and the foreign income component in the price of import substituting commodities may be high enough to raise doubts whether such productions afford a net gain to the economy as a whole. So even if a shift in foreign trade is clearly visible, this constitutes in the very small economy no conclusive proof that development is on its way.

An other type of change in the composition of foreign trade may occur in exports. The integration of production stages beyond the primary in home-produced commodities that were formerly exported in the raw spells progress. Beyond that, any broadening of the spectrum of exports betters the chances of eventually attaining a balance between the needs and availability of foreign exchange.

However promising such developments may be, they should never be judged in isolation. The apparent fact of an addition to national income may always be offset or even nulllified by simultaneous other changes. Transfers abroad, not only of profits by foreign entrepreneurs, but also of gains by other interested parties, should never be overlooked. Not in advance in feasibility studies, and not afterwards in taking corrective steps, if a too great part of the benefits is leaking away.

Changes in the composition of foreign trade may not only follow changes in production and consumption, but can also result from changes in rules and regulations. But that is not the way to provide for this aspect of transformation. Export by decree is madness, as the foreign buyers don't have to go by your book. That leaves only imports to be tampered with. But the less free trade is, the more profitable becomes circumvention of the rules. The rising costs of enforcement of the restrictions will eat into the benefits that were sought. Prices, quantities and qualities of artificially scarce goods become the explicit concern of government, that even may have to organize their distribution. And that would amount to an invitation of black marketeering. The government of a very small state is well advised to beware of overreaching itself in the field of economics.

Next on Demas' checklist is the reduction of dualism, which seems to imply a succesful combat of poverty. As long as there are, in a society, people who for the bare fact of their continued existence have to make a living somehow, while to them the regular sources of income are closed, it will be impossible to eliminate the informal sector. To wipe out poverty in a less developed society must, alas, be considered a too lofty aim, as even in the most highly developed economies of this world poverty is not a thing of the past. But this very fact may also be taken as proof that incomplete succes in wiping out poverty is in itself no insurmountable barrier to development. What seems to be important is that dualism should be reduced to proportions compatible with unchallenged prominence of the formal sector. If the informal sector is not too much of a drain on productive forces and tax receipts, its existence will slow down progress, but will not block it.

We should not lose sight of the fact that, next to poverty, greed is an important root of the informal sector. The craving for untaxed income is positively correlated with the heigth of one's tax bracket. In many economies, large and small, developed and backward, there is an elusive undercurrent of transactions ranging from secretive through shady and dark to downright criminal, all having in common that the proceeds are virtually tax free. If in an economy a sizeable proportion of the money circulation is bound up in an underground circuit, this constitutes a feedback mechanism, prompting further ventures in this field, as this may the logical way to invest the ill gotten gains.

If in a very small economy, next to its own currency, foreign exchange is also freely circulating amongst its residents, this enlarges the scope for transactions in the informal sector. This is the actual situation in the Netherlands Antilles. Though it may be deemed the right policy to link the external value of one's currency to that of the U.S. dollar, this does not mean that 'technical' domestic circulation of greenbacks is unavoidable. To ban home circulation of foreign exchange will pay for itself, because the additional amount of own currency to be circulated to take its place may be seen as a loan without interest of the public to the central bank.

One might suppose that job creation in the formal sector would in itself be enough to draw labour from the informal sector. But it is doubtful that this would be the case across the board. Thriving parts of the informal sector will remain highly attractive, especially to the ones that have become habituated to life without a steady job. The informal sector is not merely a matter of shortage of formal jobs, but also of alienation. Education towards better understanding of the values and goals of society may be in order to counter alienation of the younger generations, in step with policies to better their chances of employment in regular jobs. Policies to curb the informal sector should be continuous and non-erratic, because sudden shifts of labour between sectors in a very small economy may cause imbalances in the labour market, that would feed social unrest detrimental to continued development.

One should never lose sight of the fact that the informal sector is part and parcel of society. In a very small society its characteristics are those of society itself. It has a personalistic fabric of relationships and contains personalistic systems of dominance, with the trappings of personal power and patronage. There is no natural law enclosing such systems in a separate compartment, so they may have roots or branches in other sectors of the community. Also, these systems are not immune from foreign infiltration. In very small economies repelling the informal sector is a tricky affair.

The seventh and last element mentioned by Demas is the development of appropriate institutions. This means instilling the habits and customs to use efficient and fair procedures in the regulation of economic and social life. It also means the (re-)organization of public life into units appropriate to execute their several tasks in a coherent framework of overall policy. Very small societies are liable on both counts to come up against a number of problems that do not, or hardly, exist in large systems, whereas on the other hand possible advantages of being small are not abundant, and may need very special circumstances to be of appreciable influence.

As to the institution of modes of thinking and action required for progress, there is a danger in copying foreign examples with too little thought for realistic adaption to the local facts of life. These are, inter alia, the small social field with its surfeit of multiple roles, ingrained attitudes toward real estate ownership versus risk bearing investments, and social stress from multiple sources seeking outlets, that may be found in antagonism to attempts at social reform. On top of this personalistic aspects of political life increase the risk that ill-timed or badly understood moves of the establishment will have unexpected repercussions. It is of paramount importance that all activities are evaluated beforehand in terms of their possible effects, not only on direct targets, but also on side-issues. As far as possible objections and their sources should be foreseen, as well as the opportunities to contribute to succes through education, information and optimal timing of the steps to be taken.

The development of institutions in the sense of centres of specific activities will have to be tailored not just to the needs and aspirations of society, but above all to its realities. If, for instance, due to geographic and demographic givens, effective customs control of all ports of entry would cost appreciably more than could possibly be recovered by the levying of import duties, the institution of a customs force would not be an asset, but a liability to government finance. Even so, these losses might possibly be offset by other gains to society, like the employment of customs officials and workers in protected import substituting industries. In cost-benefit analysis of this particular problem it should however be recognized that import duties are not a levy on foreign producers, but on one's own consumers.

There is far more to the regulation of international trade, in an institutional sense, than an adequate customs force. Import licensing and price control, in line with the objectives of economic policy, require the availability of an adequately equipped and competent staff. Factors limiting the size of such a bureau, e.g. available accomodation, manpower and funds, will at the same time, though less visible, limit the effective scope of its activities. If proper execution of official policies exceeds this scope, trimming the policies may be a better medicine than expanding the bureau to an outsize out of line with local proportions and likely to lead to a lowering of standards through bureaucratisation and increasingly difficult recruitment of suitable workers, once the bottom of the barrel has been scraped.

The examples given may be supplemented by many others, for instance in the fields of education, health, social security and central banking. In a small society the production of collective and quasi-collective goods is likely to have a high unit cost, caused by diseconomies of small scale. In very small countries, especially if their territory is scattered over a number of islands, these costs may be structurally too high ever to be met by own current revenue. In these cases the people will have to live without rather basic facilities, or the costs exeeding local possibilities will have to be met *permanently* from outside sources. Such transfers should not be termed 'development funds' because the development perspective is not present. Neither should they be termed 'charity', as the right name is 'human rights transfers'. The case for international redistribution of income ultimately rests on international law.

There is good sense in regional cooperation in the development of institutions. But here the problems may be hardly smaller, and the distances will anyway be a lot larger. For instance, the area covered by the South Pacific Commission consists of twenty countries, scattered over thousands of islands. Excluding Papua New Guinea they have appreciably less than two million inhabitants, thinly spread over approximately ninety thousand square kilometers of land. This land is only one third of one percent of the total area. The rest is water. In favour of regional solutions is however the enhanced possibility to attract outside finance to cover their costs.

This has brought us to the end of Demas' list of seven points, but by no means exhausted the catalogue of development problems particular to very small societies. But for the present I am inclined to rest the case, with the exception of one final element that I have come to regard as crucial to the development process.

That apocryphal eighth point is *the removal of livability constraints on the honouring of human rights.*

The arguments for the linking of human rights to the goals of development, through dependence of the scope for the former on physical requirements covered by the concept of livability, have been given earlier, and will not be repeated here.

The equation of full development and the absence of physical barriers to the realisation of human rights, classes such barriers as underdevelopment and as legitimate explicit targets for strategies, plans and projects aimed at their removal.

The elementary individual right to the basic necessities of life, in terms of food, shelter, clothing, health care and education must certainly be considered under the heading of human rights, but also many further reaching matters, that in developed countries have attained the status of inalienable basic individual rights. If equal treatment for males and females is no more than right for Europeans, why not for Asians and Africans? Inasfar as mundial inequality affords the material scope in Europe for such social developments, there ought to be at least some reluctance to accord new formal rights to, in a global context, already privileged groups, if such rights would amount to further privileges over comparable groups elsewhere.

It is extremely important that the livability constraints on the effectuation of human rights should be made explicit by research. Once this has been done it is quite clear that many requests for development aid could be backed by justifiable claims based on internationally accepted norms of human rights. This way also the needs for permanent international income transfers in cases when endogeneous final solutions are clearly impossible, could be given a firm base in international law and be stripped of their overtones of charity.

Particularly the group of very small nations, lacking push and power in international politics, would be likely to benefit from this new approach. It seems to be in their best interest to give top priority to, and institute mutual cooperation in projects aimed at clear and unambiguous description of the levels of livability in all very small countries. In these projects much attention should be given to the selection of indicators significant for the marking of physical barriers to the realisation of human rights.

6.

VIABILITY

"How can one talk about the economics of small independent countries? How can one discuss a problem that is a non-problem? There is no such thing as the viability of states or nations, there is only a problem of viability of people: people, actual persons like you and me, are viable when they can stand on their own feet and earn their keep."

This is a statement that was made by E.F. Schumacher, in Chapter 5 of his bestseller "Small is Beautiful". I most heartily disagree. By extension of his own argument, a group of people is viable when it can stand on its own feet and earn its keep. A state or a nation IS a group of actual persons like you and me, that is sovereign in its own territory and that runs its own affairs through the institutions of its government. If this group in unable to earn its keep, which includes the costs of its institutions, it may be formally independent, but in fact it is dependent on those who are in control of the flows of funds from outside. Whether these outsiders are paternalistic idealists or greedy extorters, or anything in between, makes no difference to the fact that THEY are in control, and not the people themselves. I would not class this as a non-problem, but then I am unable to blind myself to the disadvantages of socio economic smallness that may be incompatible with romantic notions of its beauty.

I am not ridiculing such feelings, for I admit that I fully share them. Among my fondest memories are those of happy days spent on little Saba in the Windwards. But I am at the same time well aware that I can afford this luxury of savouring to the full the beauty of smallness only because I am an outsider. To those inside small may be a beautiful pain in the neck.

A life should be worth living. Also Schumacher, as quoted above, did not equate the viability of an actual person with nothing but a death risk smaller than one in the short period, but implied human dignitity in the requirement that one should be able to earn one's own keep.

What IS one's keep? In a broad sense it is the *livability* of one's life in all its material and immaterial aspects, insofar as these are dependent on the means that are spent on them. Livability may be modeled as a vector of quantifiable indicators of factors influencing the quality of life, under the restriction of the total of means to be spent in the creation, improvement and maintenance of these factors. To earn one's keep is the ability to provide this total of means as the fruits of one's own productive efforts. Thus viability in a human sense is closely linked to the livability of human life. The material requirements of the various livability factors for all individuals are in their aggregate the touching stone for viability.

Is there a physical *minimum* to this aggregate? A moment's thought is enough to see that below a certain level the sheer physical requirements for biological survival are lacking, and human life cannot be sustained. But at or just above this point life is hardly worth living, even if physically possible. From this position we have only one little step to take to the statement that the livability aggregate should afford people the scope to live humanly worth while lives. We should recognise that all human beings are naturally entitled to the opportunity to live in a human way. This feeling is at the back of the notion of fundamental human rights.

So there is a natural connection between the physical requirements for the effectuation of human rights and its associated relative minimum of the livability aggregate. But the other way round we can also point out that there is a ceiling for fundamental human rights. They could never include the right to a diamond-studded massive golden crown for every man, woman and child, simply because there is not enough to go around. The ceiling of human rights is dependent on the mundial total of resources, the number of people and the distribution of resources, interpersonal and intertemporal. Its *maximum* is associated with equal distribution of ownership and income over humanity present and future, and therefore is only a theoretical magnitude. Even so we should keep in mind that it is not a constant, as it is subject to exogeneous forces and all interdependencies between humanity and its terrestrial environment.

From this dazzling and unattainable height we step down again to the reality of a world full of inequalities. Though we admit the impossibility of making rapid fundamental changes in this sorry scheme of things, it is at least within our power to map the course of present and future generations in the direction of a world that offers accces to a truly human life to all. In that world, and in the approach toward it, the concept of human rights is bound to converge to the point where the rights of any individual balance with the equal rights of all other individuals. Also, at this point of equilibrium, its associated livability vector will be subject to the physical constraints that were formulated above. Therefore it is right now possible to make first estimates of at least some elements of the livability aggregate associated with the future human rights equilibrium. For instance, one might estimate its component of yearly pro capita energy consumption.

That estimate, even with very wide margins of error, will show that in the present world many people are forced to do with much less, whereas others are given to overconsumption. Or, of this high energy consumption is really necessary for the latter to live humanly rewarding lives, the same has to be true for the former. In that case total available energy should be increased to a level where these shares were possible for all, or the total population would have to be reduced to a level where humanly viable life would be in reach of all survivors. This in itself would of course be utterly inhuman.

For the moment this ought to be enough as a first look at the grim implications of the link between viability, livability and human rights on a world scale. It is against this terrifying background that we must make our judgments on viability in the actual cases where they are required. A fair example is the question of the viability as an independent state of a former colony. As I studied the case of the Netherlands Antilles, for me it is handy to use this example, though it does not afford me pleasure to put into writing several matters that are, as I know quite well, disheartening to those who really care about this emerging nation.

Twice in 1977 I visited the six islands in the Caribbean that constitute the Netherlands Antilles, with a main interest in its international trade, but attempting not to overlook other information that might help me to understand the economic realities and potentialities in that part of the world. My report was submitted early in 1978 and served, with some extensions but virtually unchanged, in the following year as a doctor's thesis. In the meanwhile I had made a third field trip to the territory to study transportation, with a report in October 1978. Parts of this were used in embellishment of the dissertation.

The focus on international trade stemmed from the philosophy that a jig saw puzzle, especially a very small one, is easiest solved by first doing the edges. Prior to '77 I had never visited the Caribbean and, owing to a very tight schedule for field work, analysis and reporting, there was no time for extensive reading. So I knew in advance that I would have to make the most of my opportunities for field observations although, because of the explicit exclusion of topics like tourism, domestic trade and the financial sector from my marching orders, the formal scope was narrow. But I am not much of a formalist, and somehow ended up with a fairly inclusive birds eye view of the Antillean economy, that has matured when later I took up the study of very small economies in general.

The Netherlands Antilles consist of two groups of three islands each, with a total land area of less than one thousand square kilometers, carrying a population of approximately one quarter of a million people. The largest three, Aruba, Curacao and Bonaire, are strung out West to East opposite the coast of Venezuela. Curacao has over two thirds of total population, Aruba has more than 60 000 inhabitants and Bonaire only eight thousand. The remaining seven percent of the territory is situated nine hundred kilometers to the North and consists of the southern part of St. Martin (pop. over 12 000),

St. Eustatius (pop. 1400) and Saba (pop. 1000). Total labour force about 80 000. Total jobs approximately 70 000. So there is a high unemployment rate, but a labour potential of only 10 000 to boost the national income by new ventures or growth of the existing ones. Labour is a bottleneck for any serious attempt to bring the economy to a selfsupporting level.

Labour, especially manual labour, is not popular, not only because of a hot climate, but also on account of social attitudes stemming from slavery, that was abolished in the middle of the previous century. Only Sabans, mostly of British stock, seem to have no visible aversion to 'slave labour', which is a source of wonderment and mirth to others.

Import duties do not exist and there is no customs force in the three northern islets. Import substituting industries are only found in the southern group. With concentrated efforts in this direction successive governments have managed to create employment for a few hundreds of people in a direction without perspectives of growth, because the home market is of a given small size, and there are no realistic prospects for export markets in industries that, in terms of inputs and techniques, might with the same degree of inefficiency be located anywhere else in the world. In a way it is lucky that import substitution has had only meagre results, as because of its high import requirements and large income leak abroad, its contributions to the domestic economy are very modest if not negative in terms of national income. The consumers pay through the nose for this left-handed boost to their economy, as the protection of these industries affords an umbrella to inflation of wages and prices, restricts free choice, and for that reason holds insufficient punishment for poor quality.

Neither is export industry a field teeming with untried opportunities. There is no comparative advantage in the availability of primary commodities, the wage level is high, and there are barriers to entry in most foreign markets that are hard to overcome. Beyond that, the labour bottleneck, already mentioned, restricts the possibilities of economic growth to a modest figure, even when very modern capital intensive techniques, with high value added per worker, are assumed.

At present the Antillean economy is in fact a highly subsidized one, with the government as the largest employer. This government is structurally unable to cover its running expenses from own current revenue. In the terminology of Carleen O'Loughlin[1] it does not meet the criterion of financial viability of political independence. Is it possible for the Antillean society ever to attain that state of bliss?

A necessary though not sufficient condition is development of the economy to a level where it is able to stand on its own feet and autonomously support the conglomerate of political decision making an executive implementation that is government. In the Antillean case this is not possible through mere expansion of the present too narrow base, as this base is not sound. It has its weaknesses and may be in for a decline in each of its major three sectors. To the extent that this happens even more new activities would be required to fill the gap, if it can be filled at all. Let us have a look at the three mainstays of Antillean economic life.

The most important complex is still the oil industry, though its employment in Aruba (Exxon) and Curacao (Shell) has dwindled to less than one third of what it was in its heyday. Both refineries are among the older in the world. As there is ample more modern refining capacity nearer to the most important markets, it is no wonder that these two plants operate well under their full capacity level. In this situation the oil companies have no strong motives to invest heavily in more up to date installations at these locations. These refineries are both doomed to increasing obsolescence. Strategies to sell out to the Antillean or Venezuelean government may logically be expected. My advice is not to buy.

Not independent of this negative development are the changes in

1) C. O'Loughlin 'Economic problems of the small West Indies islands' in: "Social and Economic Studies", March 1962 pp. 44 - 56.

the transportation of crude oil. As mammoth tankers could not find berth in the rather shallow ports of the North American East coast, it was efficient to use these ships to transport oil from the Middle East to tank parks near deep water in the Caribbean, whence smaller ships transported it to the United States. Such oil terminals were installed on all three islands of the Southern group. The construction of a fourth one was started on St. Eustatius in the Northern group.

This increased efficiency of crude oil transportation made it more attractive to have the refineries nearest to the markets run at full capacity, to reduce the need for importation of refinery products. The resulting redistribution of excess refining capacity was to the disadvantage of the two Antillean plants. But this is only part of the story. Technical change does not stop, and further developments soon threatened to make the recently installed oil terminals obsolete before their time.

Methods came in use to pump oil from large to smaller ships directly while at sea. Cheap bulk transportation could be extended to locations much nearer to the final destination. The smaller tankers for the last lap had a much shorter way to go, and could now complete several trips in the time and at the cost it took them formerly to make one. Further economies were found in the use of oil lighters drawn by tug boats, near the mouth of the Mississippi. The saving in transportation costs was so high that even reduction to a level far below cost of the oil terminal tariffs would not be enough to compensate for it. But somehow business went on.

Part of the business is due to the hurricane season, when trips to the Gulf of Mexico entail additional dangers for unwieldy super tankers. But there must be more to it. The terminals on Curacao and Aruba belong to oil multinationals and, as operations within large concerns are far from transparant, the lack of outward signs of distress was not particularly surprising. Not so with the oil terminal on Bonaire, that is jokingly called 'a hotel for oil' and offers its services to all. They are still in business, so there must be money somehow in detouring oil through its tank park, even if this *increases* transportation costs.

One may well wonder at the nature of this business, which is a distortion of efficiency in physical distribution that can, on logical grounds, only be profitable if it obscures an other distortion that influences costs and yields still more in the opposite direction. Therefore, whatever it is, it cannot possibly be a sound and legitimate basis for future prosperity. At the same time and for the same reasons, it is not at all clear what the present function is of the oil terminals on both other islands. I, for one, will need a lot of convincing before I could be brought to believe that they will be assets to the Antillean economy in a somewhat longer perspective. The construction of the terminal on St. Eustatius was suspended and I have had no word that it has been resumed since.

So much for the liquid black gold. Next in importance is the tourist business. Increasing numbers of holiday makers have found, from the sixties on, their way to the islands. The Caribbean is the area that is best suited in the whole world for high turnover cruise tourism.

When passenger lines lost the competition with ever safer, bigger, faster and cheaper aircraft, many proud large ships would have been in for breaking up, but for a boom in cruising. However, this boom was accompanied by a shift from exclusive and expensive arrangements for the wealthy to mass tourism within the reach of a broad middle class. As passenger shipping as a mode of transportation and accomodation is in itself inefficient, cruises remained a fairly expensive way to spend one's holidays. This means that when going ashore in a port of call, easily ten times in different places within a fortnight, many present day cruise tourists have not much money to spend. I found it a weird sight to encounter groups of elderly people walking for miles in the tropical heat of day to save taxi fares. Locals told me it was quite common. Increase of cruise tourism in this vein is not likely to bring great prosperity.

Will there be an increase? The bulk of the present trade is carried by ships that were built as passenger liners. Since they exist, it is efficient to use them as long as they show a yield exceeding running expenses and upkeep. To build similar new ships is a quite different matter, as the investment will have to be recovered. If such ships, or their modern equivalents, are built again, they are not likely to break even in their amortisation periods if there is a slack in the cruise market or a significant shift in the preferences of holiday makers. A stiffening of the competition is far from impossible. There are some smaller ships, built as car ferries, now participating in Caribbean cruising. Possibly these ships accomodate summer holiday peaks in Europe during the Caribbean off-season.

Tourists coming to the islands for stop-over holidays were formerly well-to-do people, who might have gone on a cruise, but happened to prefer less mobile surroundings. As enough is never enough, more and more hotels were built, optimistically in advance and excess of expected increases in stay-over tourism. But as soon as new accomodation is available there is a short time efficiency in using it at a discount instead of accepting a very high vacancy rate during the first years. Once this is done there is no way back. Tour operators sprang up to reap what others had too hastily sown and, as profits per tourist declined, the building of still more and bigger hotels was officially sanctioned and supported with development funds, in the hope to make good eventually through increases in total turnover. As there are too many places in the world where similar ends are pursued just as unwisely, the tour operators find their power to pick and choose increased by a plethora of possibilities to switch almost overnight from one destination to an other. But they are up against a stiffening competition amongst themselves, as they cannot bar new tour operators from entering the field. Their fight for market shares puts the prices under pressure. I heard complaints about tour operators paying much too late or not in full, for accomodation and meals that were delivered on credit. For a small island, any small island, there is no dependable economic future in mass tourism on these terms.

Disappointingly low spending per day by average North American 'package deal' holiday makers is in Aruba and Curacao offset in part by an increase in 'shopping tourism' from the southward continent, mainly from Venezuela. Increasing prosperity in South America, if not for all at least for an expanding middle class, and marked differences in the level of consumer prices, notably in textiles, are the main factors behind it. The latter aspect originates in sloppy South American official thinking on the benefits of import substitution in the face of comparative disadvantage. In the Antilles the price level is strongly influenced by unhindered cheap imports from the Far East (for instance guyabara's, a kind of open shirt with four pockets, that is worn over the trousers, at $ 12.– a dozen c.i.f), luring ever more shoppers from the continent below. Yet in an assessment of long term economic development it would be rather frivolous to expect gross distortions in international trade to carry over into the next century.

South American shopping tourism does not extend all the way to St. Martin, but this island is much nearer to the U.S. middle class mass tourism. Even low-spending vacationers amount to a sizeable turnover when they are herded together in such a small place. So at least one of the six islands may be able to get by just on tourism for an indefinite period. Lucky enough for them, as hardly anything else looks feasible on St. Martin.

The third mainstay of the contemporate Antillean economy is rooted in its mild fiscal climate, coupled to convenient international agreements acquired under the safe umbrella of the Netherlands. The Antilles are a first class tax haven, and a handful of fortunate people have a landslide business, with few exceptions only on Curacao, to administer the paper headquarters of throngs of companies that have found the loopholes to go international in order to evade taxes at home. Their multitudes are so great that, even at a ludicrously low rate of the profit tax, in the aggregate their contribution to the Antillean national income ranks third. But the employment provided by this 'sector' is insignificant and its direct contribution to activity in the domestic private sector does not differ very much from zero. There is a small indirect contribution in a fringe of financial services and banking, that is associated with it. In time this might become the nucleus of a development in Curacao as a financial center for the hemisphere.

But that is far from probable. Indeally, a financial hub has the stability, or rather the inertia, that is afforded by the sheer mass of a large system. To a certain extent this condition is provided at present through the linkage with the Netherlands, which country, fairly small in itself, is firmly embedded in Europe. The inertia will turn into volatility when the link is loosened. It will at the same time reduce the attractiveness of the Antilles as a tax haven. Also nations now faced with a steady loss of revenue because of seepage to the Antilles through links of paper, are looking for ways and means to stop the drain. It is to be expected that they will be less than eager, to say the least of it, to renew agreements on double taxation when this comes up as a corrolary to full independence. When the tide turns the government will lose a lot of revenue, and have to face the fact that rows of files in accounting offices in Willemstad afford no grip whatsoever on the vast array of foreign companies they represent, as it is too cheap and easy to hedge against importunities through other letter-boxes in other tax paradises.

Summa summarum: the three-legged Antillean economy is not firm on its feet. It will have to grow new legs if it is to serve as the carrier of an independent political superstructure. Even if these new legs can be grown the economy will not be able to stand on them before they have matured. Barred outright miracles, the Antillean economy will not be viable in its own right well into the next century. A non-viable economy cannot offer the sound tax base that is indispensable to balance aggregate running expenditures against running income. Formal independence may slightly veil, but cannot hide that no Antillean government can possibly be its own boss for many years to come.

Suppose now that, indeed by miracle, the Antillean economy becomes strong and sturdy overnight. Would that clear away the obstacles on the road to freedom? Alas not. In this respect a viable economy is a necessary, but not a sufficient condition. Even a healthy and booming economy may fall short as a source of revenue. What price independence?

To see this more clearly we will take a closer look, and give attention to three strategic magnitudes with respect to the balance of expenditures against revenue. Hardly surprising, the first of these is the level and rate of growth of government spending. The higher it is and the faster it grows, the more difficult will be its matching by revenue. The second magnitude is national income, representing the source of revenue. The third strategic magnitude is the rate at which this source may be tapped, or should we say bled: the aggregate tax rate.

First and foremost: government spending and the factors behind its level and mutations. The great culprit is small scale. Citizens of a very small state have the same needs for government, education, health and social services as the citizens of a large nation. Also, maybe not necessarily so, the government, social and other services and institutions and the whole bureaucracy are more often than not modeled after the examples of well ordered but much larger western societies. The number of agencies, institutions and bureaus in very small states tends to be out of proportion compared to the size of the system. Also, given a minimum size below which it is not possible to operate a bureau or any other institution, the number of clients per center of activity is too low for efficiency, or, conversely, the basic work load is too small. This is offset by a tendency to fill up this slack, both by eager managers and by minor officials seeking to increase their job security by not appearing idle. The organizations tend to become cluttered up with side issues and trifles, after some time even hardly able to fulfill their primary tasks efficiently. So they expand. Government and affiliated organizations in very small countries are generally by far the largest source of employment, setting narrow limits to potential expansion of the private sector and national income. For instance, in Rarotonga (Cook Islands) the *private* employment in 1980 was not even fourtythree percent of total employment, which is almost unbelievable in a free market economy. As far as my information reaches, only in Tonga the government pursues a deliberate policy of multiple assignments to its office holders, to counteract the tendency to bureaucratic growth. I know far too little about the results of this policy to commend it, but it may work.

The general case is that, even under normal concepts of organization and efficiency, the collective and social sectors of very small nations tend to be outsize in a relative sense, and thus on a pro capita base much more expensive than their counterparts in larger systems. In the Antillean case, and in other multi-island states, there is the additional disadvantage of decentralization of already inefficiently small institutions, or great problems in reaching the public they are supposed to serve. If all services are provided on each island, all disadvantages of small scale would be aggravated by further reduction of the scale, and multiplied by the number of islands. Centralization on one island still leads to the necessity of local representation on the other islands. Also lack of amenities in a semi-autonomous periphery frequently leads to local initiatives to fill gaps. This complicates the organizational structure and creates overlaps in competence, leading to unwieldy and lengthy procedures. This is a source of political tensions between the islands. It is easy to find examples in particular fields, like education and health care. The choice is between three evils:

a. a too thinly but evenly spread low level of services,
b. an acceptable level of services on each island at prohibitive cost, or,
c. concentration of all but the most basic services in one place, entailing the subsidy of inter island travel and the accomodation of sojourn away from home for students and patients.

On top of this, there are inefficiencies that, at least in the opinion of an outsider, might have been avoided in the first place and ought to be remedied where they have taken root. If the purpose of excess government employment is the provision of income to the workless, a negative judgment should possibly not be passed until after a careful consideration of all arguments and a cost-benefit analysis that does not overlook the alternative costs of unemployment to society. Not so however when government sinecures are given to political friends or their kin as rewards in the context of systems of patronage. This inefficient use of communal funds detracts from the prospects of financially viable independence.

The example of developed societies also tends to boost government expenditure. With respect to collective and quasi-collective goods, the level of aspiration in the Netherlands Antilles is high. This is reflected in the infrastructure. Because it was possible and even relatively easy to have infrastructural investments financed with aid funds, there has been a propensity to overinvestment, losing sight of the running costs of exploitation and upkeep these investments entailed. A glaring example of this is found in the main road system of Curacao. It includes a four lane bridge high over Anna Bay, that reminds one of San Francisco, but was not needed to get from one end of the island to the other. The biggest pearl in this network of speedways, with its loops, viaducts and the latest in traffic lights, is a truly gigantic crossing north east of the harbour, where a pedestrian has either to be an accomplished athlete or has to hire a car to cross it safely. Very aptly this crossing is called 'Biesheuvel', which happens to be the name of a former Netherlands prime minister, who subsequently became chairman of the endlessly dragging on round table talks on Antillean independence. This crossing is indeed the ideal monument for the obstacles that, with our generous help, have been placed on the road to independence.

There is a strong connection between road construction and the increase of traffic. The density is extremely high and still increasing. Satiation is expected round 1990 at a level of 310 vehicles per thousand residents, excluding trucks and buses. This exceeds the theoretical satiation level of very large metropolitan western cities. There is no need to spell out all costs to society of this disproportionate development to conclude that it is in a dramatic way detrimental to the level of government spending. Also in various other respects, for instance sea- and airports, the infrastructure is out of harmony with the endogeneous carrying capacity and stands no chance ever to break even on its own revenue, e.g. harbour dues and landing fees.

In this all there certainly has been no deliberacy from either side to block independence in some Machiavellian fashion. On the contrary, the good intentions are abundantly clear. It is just that projects proportionate to their surroundings in very small societies look in the planning phase so ridiculously small to outsiders. The merest vestige of paternalism in those controlling aid funds would be enough to make them object to what looks to them like the frittering away of money. There usually is more than a vestige of paternalism and the recipient of aid anticipates this and does not even try. To get aid one has to majorate.

Once such developments are realised they cannot be undone. Only marginal readjustments remain possible. In the case of a new project, though, the foreseeable influence on the budget should carry a heavy weight in the investment decision. That is, if one really wishes to go independent. Such care, however, is in the case of the Netherlands Antilles not to be expected. On the contrary, there will be a proclivity to obtain parting gifts from the former colonial overlord in the form of further projects entailing recurring expenses in excess of yields. Government spending and its trend are and will remain a disequilibrating factor.

The source of domestic revenue to match running expenditures is our next concern. The national income of a very small country cannot be expected to expand to a level beyond its potential. Its productive forces are restricted and its resources are limited. We may clarify the position by the formal equation of national income with the total number of jobs times the average value added per worker. The actual variation in value added per job performed is, of course, great. Increases of national income would result from shifts of labour from occupations with low to activities with high value added. But the scope for such operations is in reality much smaller than in models. The mean of per capita value added will change only slowly and will not rise to a spectacular level in the next score of years. What will be the position beyond that time horizon nobody can tell, but dramatic changes remain improbable.

The other factor is the labour force, that is in the order of roughly one third of the population. As was argued in an earlier chapter, it has been drained by emigration of part of its prime members. Only the unemployed, containing a subgroup of unemployable, are available for a quick boost of the volume of production, but even at a high rate of unemployment, say twice the actual present rate, the labour reserve would be too small in absolute numbers for ambitious growth targets. Neither in the utilisation of labour, nor in a boost of average value added is the scope for fast and sustained growth of national income to be found.

Removing the labour bottleneck through immigration is not impossible, but it has serious drawbacks. To generate a worthwhile impact on the national income the number of immigrants would have to be sizeable. They would claim living space in places that are already densely settled. They would have to be not just manual labourers, but highly qualified persons, to perform jobs in the vanguard of technological advance, as the avowed purpose is a boost of national income. Such workers are in demand also in other places. Consequently they will demand high wages, which tends to pull the local wages structure out of true and give rise to tensions in the labour market. Historical examples of this mechanism are abundant.

If the immigrants are permanent or on long term contracts they will bring their families along, and this will result in exclusion of autochthones from many attractive jobs. If the immigrants are brought in on contracts for strictly limited short periods, their payroll will benefit the economy only to a little extent, because of savings abroad and support of dependents in the home country. In Liechtenstein, where industrialisation was accompanied by immigration from the neighbouring states and daily streams of foreign commuters, the official enthousiasm for this way to achieve economic growth has declined. It is hardly to be expected that on a similar policy a Caribbean very small society would fare much better.

To utilize available labour with optimal efficiency is a hard nut to crack, as rapid technological change in fact constantly threatens all contemporate production processes with untimely obsolescence. This danger is greatest in import substitution. Production only for a very small home market demands appropriate techniques, as the costs of underutilisation tend to nullify economies of scale. New techniques speed up or broaden the potential production stream and, at the ceiling of home demand for the product, only raise the level of underutilisation. The idea to produce at full capacity and export the surplus is wholly naive and unrealistic for goods without comparative advantages to offset the costs of their marketing and delivery in places where the same goods can be produced with the same or even higher efficiency.

Obsolete import substitution can, of course, be continued almost indefinitely by a ban or prohibitive duties on competing imports. In that case one's own consumers are duped. Through inflated prices they provide a subsidy for the sub-optimal utilisation of labour and the featherbeds of marginal employers. If this comes to pass, which would not be so unique, import substitution is not an asset, but a liability to society.

Even when such industries are ostentatiously healthy, one may have one's doubts. As invariably inputs have to be imported, and foreign ownership and management are frequent, the foreign exchange component in market prices of their products is surprisingly high. A large part of value added leaks abroad, leaving scanty profit for the domestic economy even in 'healthy' cases. I have remarked on this in my dissertation, with reference to a number of plants in Curacao and Aruba.

Chances to produce goods and services for export are habitually far from abundant in places where neither natural nor man-made comparative advantages are outstanding. Also, in the volatile system of an economy lacking the inertia of mass, the initial risks are great. Even with the most painstakingly careful forethought, failures are to a certain extent unavoidable. They must be weathered without too much disappointment, because only by perseverance, creativity, flexibility and a talent to make the most of any lucky breaks will it at all be possible to arrive at a reasonably sound economic foundation for the Antillean society. Even in the most optimistic scenario that will take more than twenty years. In the intervening years growth of national income, even if spectacular in some respects, will not be enough for the purpose of true independence.

It now remains to be seen how this source may be tapped to the best interests of society. Some prudence is in order, but there should not be too much reluctance to levy taxes and demand proper contributions for social benefits. If we lump all sources of domestic revenue together in the term 'aggregate tax rate', our first observation is that in the Antilles it is rather low, compared to its counterpart in many other countries.

Compared to my own country, both direct and indirect tax rates are on the low side. I was really bowled over to find that there was no excise on petrol in Curacao and Aruba, but an import duty further strengthening the local monopolies of the two multinational refineries. Excise on tobacco wares, booze and beer were low. Numerous other commodities were not touched by excise, whereas the tariffs of the import duties did not indicate a compensation for this lack. Import duties tend to be low anyway and are altogether unknown in the Windwards up north.

This situation is of long standing. Though it is favourable to South American shopping tourism, it preceded the boom so long that we may see it as a fortitious consequence and not as the original aim of a deliberate policy. The lack of any strong urgency to cover expenses from own revenue is much more likely to have been the moving, or should we say the retarding force.

Conscpicuous is the readiness and at times even eagerness of the Antillean semi-independent government to be overgenerous with potential tax receipts. I repeatedly met the fallacy that tax holidays are an efficient instrument to promote employment and contribute to development in one stroke. As the reduction of unemployment is pursued as a short term aim, whereas development needs a structural vision, the clash of these inconsistent policy aims is in itself a good explanation of the poor record of economic progress in these islands over the past twenty years.

Even if the policy of mainly promoting import substitution itself had been above reproach, the instrument of tax favours should not have been used, as it is inefficient as such and detrimental in the end, when the expiration of the tax holiday inspires island hopping to the next tax fools paradise, which is facilitated by a stiff competition in Santa Claus lures between sloppy-thinking governments.

Research, not just recently, but over the last twenty or thirty years, has shown consistently that tax favours do not constitute a strong lure for potential investment. A number of other factors, part of which is equally in reach of government manipulation at lower costs, ranks higher than the prospect of saving on taxes if and only if profits are made. This is not at all strange. It stands to reason that level headed businessmen will always put first things first, and assign major weight to factors influencing expectations of initial losses, and the risk assessment over the amortisation period. No sane entrepreneur will prefer uncertain tax savings in a risky setting over the prospect of paying moderate taxes over profits that may be expected with confidence. Of course, if one has this confidence there is no point in declining tax favours when they are offered.

The function of tax holidays is to influence the choice between equally attractive locations and at times induce replanning of the amortisation period in step with the duration of the tax holiday. Its cost is not zero, though this is often lightheartedly argued by politicians and executives, who like to compare the tax effects to the case if there had been no investment and, consequently, no benefits at all. However, the right comparison is with a case when the investment has been made without a tax holiday, but with fairly inexpensive attention to aspects crucial to the choice of the location. That kind of improvement is in the nature of a comparative advantage over non-improved locations elsewhere, and therefore contributes to the viability of the economy. The objection against tax holidays does not rest only on its fiscal aspects. It is too easy to be healthy.

In the Antillean fiscal practice examples big and small are to be found of an easygoing attitude, giving precedence to the saving of trouble over the saving of revenue. Also, not altogether independent of this, there is a sizeable inofficial circuit, fed by transactions ranging from shady through grey and black to downright criminal. Incomes in the informal sector, no matter how heterogeneous, have in common that they are neither taxed nor subject to contributions for social benefits. A flourishing inofficial circuit is likely to boost its own further growth, if its circulating funds are easier put into further informal ventures than in the formal sector, where their emergence in a society with little anonymity would call for explanations.

Our general conclusion can be that in the Antilles the scope for an increase in tax and social premium receipts is considerable. If the other two strategic magnitudes would not prevent it, this might provide the leverage to attain viable independence. But it should be borne in mind that this cannot possibly be achieved by passing some laws, but only through lengthy processes of social change. For many years to come there is no way in which a formally independent Antillean government will be able to meet its recurrent expenditures from own revenue. As he who pays the piper calls the tune, there will not be real independence from outside powers in the near and not so near future.

There is much in this case that is bound to be relevant to other very small nations. In our world, with its given power structures and wealth-oriented norms and values, that are behind the dictum of financial viability of independence, there may in this respect be only gradual differences between them. Maybe they could in coming years improve their position by mutual cooperation aimed at weakening and eventually breaking the link between outside money and inside decision making. This might be done through the intermediary of an international organization of their own, under the blue umbrella of the United Nations. A starting point for that development could be organization of a systematic exchange of information.

Meanwhile, much more fundamental changes in human relationships are needed, not just for the very small, but for all, if mankind is to survive for an indefinite length of time in a humanly acceptable way on this planet. A possible approach, that appears to be both comprehensible and applicable, is contained in the use of the connection between human rights and livability, that is at the heart of the matter of human viability.

I seldom give credits and expect none. I do not have the time or inclination to trace the conception, birth and growth of thoughts behind my writings, but I am morally sure that none of them is original. If there appears to be some novelty in the way I have put the pieces together, that must be because none of us reads all that has been written. Anyway, common sense belongs to all of us, and to nobody in particular. In my attempts at analysis of the viability problems of very small nations I have stumbled on a way of looking at economic problems that was novel to me. Whether it IS new or old is not relevant. Now that I have come across it I have shouldered the consequences of my convictions. For me economics must be the science of provision of the wherewithal of humanly acceptable life to mankind present and future.

Linking human rights to the livability of human life entails a major shift in economic thinking, from the common absurd perspective of infinitive progress projected on a finite system, to a quasi-cardinal analysis of the possibilities and impossibilities of human life in its circumscribed environment.

The physical requirements for a right life for all, in an ethically acceptable sense, exceed the minimum requirements of bare biological viability to such an extent that the resulting total claim of present mankind on world resources, constituting the lower limits of a humanised society, may be dangerously high in some of its elements, compared to the potentialities of this world. These potentialities are the overall ceiling to the aggregate of possible claims of man on the material supports of livability. It is up to, amongst many others, the economists of this world to help prevent that present and future generations get crushed between floor and ceiling of the scope for human life.

Modeling of the concept of a bounded realm for human existence, within which all aspects of problems of interpersonal and intertemporal distribution may, mutually consistent and operational, be brought into focus, deserves high priority to be developed as a general setting for all partial economic thinking contained in existing theories and models. Not only in order to debunk chimeral schemes aimed at targets outside the circumscribed realm, but also to make explicit any current and future attempt to favour certain groups or generations at the cost of others, by activities changing the place and form of the bounds of human existence. All economic processes, in particular those purposely conceived by governments to change economic and social life, should be judged against the background of their respective process spaces, which are sub-spaces of the human realm, in order to see to it that they are consistent with the ultimate goal of a humanised mundial society.[2]

Neither a prophet nor a teacher, not even a theorist, but a flat-footed empiricist turning in disgust his broad back on a chimeral quest for infinite material progress within the finite physical system of a small planet, has stumbled over what Lin Yu Tang called 'The Importance of Living', with its twin faces viability and livability, and the strong link between the latter and fundamental human rights, opening a vista on a promised land none of us will enter, yet setting us the task to mark the road toward it for future generations. Mini-economic analysis of viability has spawned the core of mega-economic theory. Les extrèmes se touchent. So be it.

2) See Annex III.

7.

EPILOGUE

An earlier version of this text was about ready for the printer near the end of 1981. Not independent of an unfortunate decision in the selection of a publisher there were unreasonable delays. Before I could redress the situation a string of adversities had effectively put an end to my hopes to carry out field work related to the subject in the remaining years before retirement. As the very purpose of my too hasty attempt at early publication had been to pave (or maybe I should say bulldozer) the way for this field work, more or less like lifting myself by my own bootstraps, I gave up in disgust and locked the manuscript away in a deep drawer, with some poems and other atrocities left over from youthful days when I had literary ambitions.

Late in 1983 I suppressed my nausea long enough to go through the manuscript again, to see if parts of it could be cannibalised for an article. I found, more or less to my surpsise, that in the intervening two years I had somehow lost my preoccupation with the burning wish to do field work in miniature economies, and found myself able to take a more mature view of the text as such, and not as an abortive means to an unattainable end. I concluded that, though it definitely required rewriting in several parts, it contained plenty that was worth to be made available to others inclined to take up the subject of economics of very small societies. Even so it took me several months to come to a decision whether I really wanted to do all this work while there was no longer any percentage in it for me. As an old age pensioner I would be out of the race after January 1985.

Once I had made up my mind there was a decision to be taken what to do with new information, that had come to hand in the meanwhile. At least part of it was quite relevant, but its optimal use would probably lead to a much more thorough overhaul of my text than I considered practicable in the limited time that was left. If I could not stick to a strict planning and there were to be any delays, this would probably mean the end of any hopes to get the thing published at all. Lucky enough my health did not bother me any more, but the unalterable deadline was October 1984 if I wanted to see the book published while I was still on the active list. And that is what I wanted. So I decided to avoid the risk to get bogged down in new and possibly still newer literature, by saving it up for this, the final, chapter. I introduce it here more or less as an afterthought without intent to use any of it as extension or embellishment of my own text. My only purpose is to make the reader aware of the existence of this documentation, thereby underlining the fact that what I have said on mini-economics is not the last or even the latest word.

In Chapter 5 mention was made of the triangle small scale – isolation – development. The word 'isolation' in its original meaning stands for a characteristic typical of islands: their insularity. That the vast majority of very small societies existing today consists of island states is not a freakish accident of history, but the confirmation of the existence of a strong relationship between isolation and socio-economic smallness. This underlines the importance for our subject of a descriptive study entitled "Viability of Small Island States". It was commissioned by the Secretariat of UNCTAD, and executed by Francois Doumenge. It is addressed at identification of geographical factors governing the life of developing island states, the determination of various aspects of political, economic and social viability of these societies and their interactions, and the assessment of the importance of these factors in the context of development policy.

Professor Doumenge's study[1] is primarily analytical and descriptive. It provides basic information, from which conclusions may be drawn

1) F. Doumenge "Viability of Small Island States" UNCTAD TD/B/950, Geneva July 1983 (mimeographed, 43 pages).

in regard to the development constraints and options with which small island states are confronted. The intimate relationship between land and sea in the environment of any island, taken as a whole, is brought out clearly.

The study includes an analysis of various dimensions of the demographic, cultural and economic viability of island states, as well as the influence on these aspects of political factors. Two aspects are deemed of crucial importance: the precarious nature of island life, and the tug of war between insularity and the need for a more open attitude. There is a fragility of insular ecosystems, akin to the vulnerability of isolated populations to the introduction of new diseases, changes in its ways of life and shifts in its modes of production.

The precarious existence of island societies is also reflected in their susceptibility to natural disasters. This brings us to an other recent report of UNCTAD, with the title "The Incidence of Natural Disasters in Island Developing Countries"[2]. The first part of this document gives information on the incidence of natural disasters in a number of island developing countries. The second part highlights the economic and social effects of natural disasters in these societies. Part three contains conclusions and recommendations. A lot of information concerning particular island states is given in 15 annexes. Part of the contents is summarized in maps and tables. The bibliography is ample.

There is clear evidence that, as a group, island developing countries are particularly exposed to natural hazards. For one thing, because many are situated in hurricane zones and geologically active areas. But possibly more important yet is the relation between the severity of a natural disaster and the extent of the area hit by it. The often overwhelming proportional impact on small island states is deemed

2) "The Incidence of Natural Disasters in Island Developing Countries", UNCTAD TD/B/961, Geneva, September 1983 (mimeo 126 p.).

to justify special concern by the international community. There is a need for the development of better disaster impact assessment techniques, disaster insurance schemes and international agreements for disaster assistance. Of great importance are adequate measures to avoid post-disaster imbalances, environmentally as well as social and economic, as these would lead to a long term increase in vulnerability to subsequent disasters.

Preparedness for disasters and disaster relief may be embedded in a managerial approach to the problems of small societies. The latter topic has been broached by Courtney N. Blackman[3]. The author states bluntly that "... the most certain road to economic ruin is the uncritical acceptance of the recommendations of international organizations." A number of his loud objections to the standard methodology of outside consultants when advicing policy makers is well taken. I heartily concur with his contempt of econometrics: "The paradox of the econometric model is that the more stable economic conditions are, the more reliable forecasts they provide; yet the more stable conditions are, the less need is there for accurate forecasts". Good forecasts in the face of discontinuities would be very nice to have, but that is precisely where the statistical approach falls on its face.

According to Blackman, the main characteristic of the text book approach, whether left or right, is the teleological nature of the analysis. "Solutions are known in advance of the analysis." In the managerial approach there is no adherence to any apriori model of the way the world ought to hang together. There is a healthy emphasis on decision making in the light of the need to exploit a multiplicity of little openings and opportunities. The managerial approach is (1) decision-oriented, (2) programme-oriented and (3) systems-oriented.

3) C.N. Blackman 'The economic development of small countries: a managerial approach' in' "Contemporary International Relations in the Caribbean" (ed. B.A. Ince), Port of Spain 1979.

Particularly the systems approach is very important, as it does away with ceteris paribus fallacies in partial analyses. "The systems approach recognises that in real life some variables do not stand still for others to change." Its focus is not primarily on the competitive aspects of society, but more on the interrelatedness of human activities. Not the tug-of-war between capital and labour, but their complementarity is the foundation of economic life, as I have argued over and over.[4]

According to Blackman, the 'managerial' economist recognizes clearly that the solution of a problem more often than not lies in the uniqueness of the case and not in its generality. Moreover he knows that he is not likely ever to come up with the 'correct' solution, but contents himself with doing better today than he did yesterday.

An interesting aspect of Blackman's paper is his flat refusal to accept small scale as an impediment to economic growth. In this respect I cannot possibly agree with his opinions, which may in part rest on his great aversion to broad generalisations. Indeed, there may be rare cases where smallness is an asset and not a liability. I even will submit an example of a possible way to profit from small size, but that in no way nullifies the fact that in a vast majority of cases socio-economic smallness is a handicap.

Chips and automation bring us new techniques, that are often less sensitive than older ones for economies of scale. At the same time they cause significant changes in the structure and level of employment. In many industrial societies their introduction meets increased resistance from labour and only halfhearted support from governments, preoccupied as they are with the political implications of social unrest. In a very small economy the same techniques may help to overcome the restrictions of the structurally small labour force, without displacing labour as the very small economy did not encom-

4) See for instance p. 33 of "A Road to Full Employment".

pass the production techniques that are being displaced outside its borders. In particular cases this may create sound opportunities for import substitution. Better yet, here we may find a comparative advantage in exports to larger countries hesitating to introduce the new techniques themselves. With this advantage in mind, foreign firms, faced with labour resistance amounting to costly introduction lags in their home countries, may be interested in setting up their new automated plants in places where no labour resistance is to be overcome, if the further costs and risks are expected to be relatively low. It stands to reason that this kind of advantage of the very small is not structural, but of a temporary nature. It can be one of the lucky breaks that should be played for what they are worth, in a dynamic context that will remain fragile and vulnerable.

Blackman points out, rightly, that the managerial approach is easiest in a small system, as in larger systems it is confronted with problems of ever greater complexity in step with greater size. His jump to the conclusion that for this reason small economies are more manageable than large ones is however not warranted, as the manageability of a system also is a function of the number of variables that is not endogeneously manageable. This number is inversely related to size, which may be concluded from the negative correlation between the size of an economy and the degree of its openness. One of the facts of life in minature states is their extreme sensitivity to exogeneous forces, well out of the reach of inside managers. All the same, the managerial approach may amount to a positive influence on the attitudes and alertness of decision makers in very small societies.

Mainly for its intriguing title I will not omit mention of H. Corkran's book "Mini-Nations and Macro-Cooperation". It deals with political issues in international relationships and is much more to the interest of the larger partners in these interactions than to the very small ones, that cannot possibly devote sufficient resources to outside representation to join in international consultations on an equal footing. Even if they did they would not have the pull to sway decisions their way. But I found Chapter 7 of this book, containing a review of the birth and subsequent history of the South Pacific Commission, very interesting.

I owe an explanation to at least some readers about whatever happened to the Small Economies Research Center, that I set up under the wings of the Economic Geographic Institute of the University of Amsterdam early in 1981, to serve as a focus for research and a transfer point for information. Well, I never managed to raise any financial support for this organization. It died from neglect during the time I was off the active list and not expected to recover. Though I am still of the opinion that mini-economics is in need of a research and information center, I have accepted the failure of my initiative, as well as the fact that I am not in a position to have a second go at it.

In hindsight somewhat too rashly I staked out my claim in a neglected corner in the field of economics, hoping for a bonanza of information on the workings of socio-economic small scale. But the more I digged, the clearer it became that the ore in this mine is far from pure, and to an appreciable extent mixed with at least two other complex components: the level of development and the degree of isolation. These three components appear to be fused together very closely. Their conglomerate will need careful and painstaking processing to separate them, in order to discover their individual properties and the nature of their interactions.

In a way, therefore, I should consider myself lucky that I am forced at this juncture to turn in a preliminary assayer's report and abandon the claim. This way I miss out on arduous work for meagre results, as for financial reasons my tools would not amount to much beyond pick and shovel. But being a digger by nature, I had to overcome feelings of bitter disappointment, since I am thoroughly convinced that 'there is gold in thar'them hills'.

I was particularly chagrined by the inability to do any more digging into the relationship between isolation and underdevelopment. I would expect to find not only a correlation between isolation and backwardness, but also between isolation and the conservation of traditional norms and values. This, if handled well, may amount to a social advantage outweighing economic arrears in some small societies, through social cohesiveness as the context for endogeneously motivated processes of change.

We may expect that in a general sense the level of livability in small states is bound up with the level of economic development. A word of warning is in order, though. One should never equate a high level of material welfare with human bliss. The quest for higher livability levels is emphatically not the pursuit of happiness when extended beyond fairly simple needs. No level of livability will satisfy people missing the ability to be happy in the first place. With this caveat, the livability concept may be developed into a handy tool for the estimation of the influence of development differentials on the daily life of people, singly or in groups. This assessment of their differences is a prerequisite for getting a clear view of that which very small nations all over the world have in common. Once that insight is gained, small peoples are bound to discover how much they stand to gain by mutual cooperation in the development of sound problem solving strategies for their particular brands of problems.

Research entailing field studies in scores of very small territories, scattered widely over our planet, is very expensive. Especially so if it has to be carried out by outside agencies. So right now there is already a strong case for cooperation in the collection and distribution of information. Time and again expensive outside expertise is brought in to invent the same wheels that have been invented already in other small places, and even may have been shown to be square instead of round. There should be a library, containing all plans, reports and feasibility studies, executed in scores of very small nations since the end of the second world war.

Maybe the library of a supra-national organization, like the South Pacific Commission, could serve as a starting point for a Small Societies Information Service on a mundial scale. Its funding should include the means for organizing the feedback of information to the contribuants. That should be all very small societies, in their own interest.

My personal opinion is, somewhat pessimistic, that the insularity of the majority of micro-states does not augur well for world wide cooperation. Even regional cooperation between such entities is fraught with obstacles. The end of the decolonisation process of the Netherlands Antilles may easily entail the end of their existence as a conglomerate political entity. In my dissertation I pointed out the rather obvious fact that their independence as one nation would imply an endogeneous mechanism of interinsular income transfers, because of the grossly unqueal interinsular distrubution of the pro capita tax base. This way the exogeneous colonial tie would be replaced by endogeneous neocolonial interdependencies. In a political field already saturated with strong insular sentiments, this would amount to not one but several breaking points. I pointed out the need for balance on a pro capita basis in the interinsular distribution of income. I even let it be known that I had definite ideas on the lines along which this goal might be pursued. however without putting my cards on the table.

At that time this secretiveness appeared to make good sense in a strategy to obtain contracts for further research in the Caribbean. My commitment to that strategy did not bear fruit however, and got me into a strange predicament, the very day and hour when I defended my thesis.

In the audience I had observed the presence of collegues associated with organizations interested in the same assignments I was after. When Professor Goedhart questioned me directly on the matter I avoided, on an impulse, to give a straight answer, understanding very well that this was bound to make a weird impression, but counting on getting away with it. I did. Barely, as I found out afterwards. I was probably saved by my staunch reputation as a hard working though erratic character. The incident unnerved me thoroughly. I went through the remainder of that day in a haze, committing some social gaffes that make me blush even now.

At the time this happened I counted on being vindicated ex post through the new assignment. When it became clear that this hope was idle, so much water had passed beneath the bridge that it was pointless to do anything else than try to forget the painful incident. But try as I might, the memory nagged on. So I wrote it all up now, in a last attempt to exorcize this evil spirit.

All the while, my solution to the problem of parallel development of the six island economies could have been duplicated by any careful reader of my thesis, because *all of its elements were there already.*

Managed enterprise zones would have to be developed in Curacao and Aruba. A large container terminal, with ample berthing capacity to become a transfer point for container shipping between Europe and Central America, and North and South America, might be built on the coast of Little Bonaire, by the way the only nautically real good location in the whole region, but not taken in account by the 'experts', as the tug-of-war in this matter, fed by strong inter-island rivalries, was between Aruba and Cucacao.

Saint Martin would have to get by somehow on its tourist trade. On Saba virtually unlimited supplies of clean and cheap geothermal energy could be tapped and exported by underseas cable. In the first place to St. Eustatius, at only 30 kilometers distance. Near the western tip of that island a cargo port might be located in Simpson Bay, and an industrial zone in the adjacent Venus Bay plain. Even fairly unpleasant industries could, within reason, be accomodated here, as the prevailing winds would carry smells and fumes over hundreds of kilometers of open sea. The same winds turn the practically empty northeastern part of the island into a near-ideal location to house ten or fifteen thousand workers. This development would raise St. Eustatius' population to approximately the same number as St. Martin's and thus make for a now unattainable interinsular political balance in this area, with little Saba well placed to tip the scales either way.

In reality developments do not follow these lines or any other approach with comparable objectives. Disintegration of the Netherlands Antilles as a political unity before the end of the century is becoming more probable by the day. Aruba has already negotiated a separate status prior to independence. This saddles Curacao with the prospect of sole responsibility for the other four islands. These four are so small in population, compared to Curacao, that they may anticipate to have precious little influence not only in national affairs, but also at home. In the meanwhile Curacao has found it expedient to emphasize its own political status by inaugurating a new flag, a 'national' anthem and a coat of arms.

Quite a few Antilleans are less than happy with what I have heard termed 'being railroaded to independence'. The prospect may be deemed so gloom that I, for one, would not ever blame any Antillean politician for stratagems to sabotage the negotiations in order to delay formal independence as long as possible. In fact, Antillean independence, now, in whatever form, may be attractive only to the Netherlands, indecently eager to liquidate the last vestiges of its colonial heritage, without real care for the people involved. The decent thing to do would be to freeze the status quo well into the next century, instead of creating now a political vacuum, that is almost sure to be filled up from the right or from the left. Surinam, Grenada, and the whole mess of Central America are signs on the wall.

To revise this text was a solitary affair, even to the point of single-handed typing and proofreading the final version. This absolves me from the tricky problem where to start and where to stop giving credits. The weak spots, faults and even the typing errors in this text are unequivocally and irrevocably my own.

I could not care less, as the completion of this book marks the end of my activities as an economist. Without regrets and beyond looking back I am ready to enter the next stage of my development as a sentient being. Or its end, as the case may be.

I

LITERATURE

Aleman, R.T. 'Die Theorie des peripherischen Wirtschaft' in: "Weltwirtschaftliches Archiv", 1955.

Baldwin, R.E. 'Secular movements in the terms of trade' in: "American Economic Review", May 1955.

Benedict, B. (ed.) "Problems of Smaller Territories", London 1967.

Benedict, B. 'Social aspects of smallness' in: "Problems of Smaller Territories" (ed. B. Benedict), London 1967.

Blackman, C.N. 'The economic development of small countries: a managerial approach' in: "Contemporary International Relations in the Caribbean" (ed. B.A. Ince), Port of Spain 1979.

Butter, A.J. "Wat heet onafhankelijk?" ('What Price Independence?'), Amsterdam 1979.

Butter, A.J. "A Road to Full Employment: an Essay on Regulation, Deregulation, Enterprise Zones and the Producibility of Jobs", Amsterdam 1983.

Chenery, H. "Redistribution with Growth" (with M.S. Ahluwa, C.L.G. Bell, J.H. Duloy and R. Jolly), Oxford 1974.

Capra, F. "The Turning Point", 1982 (paperback edition London 1983).

Corkran, H. "Mini-Nations and Macro-Cooperation", Washington, D.C.

Demas, E.G. "The Economics of Development in Small Countries", Montreal 1965.

Doumenge, F. "Viability of Small Island States", TD/B950 UNCTAD Geneva 1983.

Emmanuel, A. "L'échange inégal", Paris 1969.

Fabricant, S. 'Study of the size and efficiency of the American economy' in: "The Economic Consequences of the Size of Nations" (ed. E.A.G. Robinson), New York 1960.

Friedeberg, A.S. "The United Nations Conference on Trade and Development of 1964", Rotterdam 1970 (2nd ed).

GEMENGDE Commissie van Nederlandse en Antilliaanse Deskundigen (= Joint Committee of Dutch and Antillean Experts) "Aanzet tot een Beleidskader", The Hague 1979.

Gevel, A.J.W. van de 'De proliferatie van modellen van de internationale handel' in: "De Economist", 119, nr.5, 1971.

Haberler, G. 'Terms of trade and economic development' in: "Economic Development for Latin America" (ed. H.S. Hillis), London 1961.

Harrison, P. "Inside the Third World", 1979 (Pelican)

Helmers, F.L.C.H. "Project Planning and Income Distribution", London 1979 (2nd ed).

Hutchison, T.W. "Knowledge and Ignorance in Economics", Oxford 1977.

INCIDENCE "The ––––– of Natural Disasters in Island Developing Countries", report TD/B/961 UNCTAD Geneva 1983.

Jacobs, J. "Cities and the wealth of nations", New York 1984.

Jencks, C. et al. "Inequality", London 1972.

Khan, A.R. "Basic Needs: an Illustrative Exercise in Identification and Quantification, with Reference to Bangladesh", ILO-paper (mimeo) Geneva 1976.

Knox, A.D. 'Some economic problems of small countries' in: "Problems of Smaller Territories" (ed. B. Benedict), London 1967.

Kohr, L. "The Overdeveloped Nations", Swansea 1976.

Kuznets, S. 'Economic growth of small nations' in: "The Economic Consequences of the Size of Nations" (ed. E.A.G. Robinson), New York 1960.

Lewis, W.A. "The Theory of Economic Growth", London 1960.

Lovelock, J. "Gaia: a New Look at Life on Earth", London/New York 1979.

Mellor, J.W. "The New Economics of Growth", London 1976.

Michaely, M. 'Concentration of imports and exports: an international comparison' in: "Economic Journal", December 1958.

Nurkse, R. "Patterns of Trade and Development", Stockholm 1959.

O'Loughlin, C. 'Economic problems of the small West Indies islands' in: "Social and Economic Studies", March 1962.

Philips, P.A.M. van "Public Finance and Less Developed Economy with Special Reference to Latin America", The Hague 1957.

Prachowny, M.F.J. "Small Open Economies", London 1975.

Robinson, E.A.G. (ed.) "The Economic Consequences of the Size of Nations", London 1960.

Rostow, W.W. "The Stages of Economic Growth", London 1960.

Rostow, W.W. 'The take-off into self-sustained growth' in: "Economic Journal", March 1956.

Seers, D. 'The mechanism of an open petroleum economy' in: "Social and Economic Studies", June 1964.

Singham, A.W. 'Legislative-executive relations in smaller territories' in: "Problems of Smaller Territories" (ed. B. Benedict), London 1967.

Viner, J. "International Trade and Economic Development", Oxford 1953.

Wallich, H.C. "Monetary Problems of an Export Economy", Harvard 1950.

Woods, D.P.J. 'The smaller territories: some political considerations' in: "Problems of Smaller Territories" (ed. B. Benedict), London 1967.

II

VERY SMALL COUNTRIES

less than 1000 inhabitants

Cocos Islands
Pitcairn
Vatican City

1000 - 2000 inhabitants

Falkland Islands
Johnston Island
Norfolk Island
Tokelau
Wake Islands

2000 - 5000 inhabitants

Christmas Island
Midway Islands
Niue Island
St. Helena
Svalbard and Jan Mayen

5000 - 10 000 inhabitants

Andorra
Nauru
St. Pierre and Miquelon
Turks and Caicos
Virgin Islands (U.K.)
Wallis and Futuna
Tuvalu

10 000 - 20 000 inhabitants

Cayman Islands
Cook Islands
Montserrat
San Marino

20 000 - 50 000 inhabitants

American Samoa
Faeroe Islands
Gibraltar
Greenland
Liechtenstein
Monaco

50 000 - 100 000 inhabitants

Antigua
Bermuda
Djibouti
Dominica
French Guiana
Grenada
Guam
Isle of Man
Kiribati
New Hebrides
St Kitts - Nevis - Anguilla
St. Vincent
Sao Tomé and Principe
Seychelles
Tonga
Virgin Islands (U.S.A.)

100 000 - 200 000 inhabitants

Belize
Brunei
Channel Islands
French Polynesia
Maldives
New Caledonia
Pacific Islands
Quatar
St. Lucia
Solomon Islands
West Samoa
Sikkim

200 000 - 500 000 inhabitants

Bahamas
Bahrain
Barbados
Cape Verde
Comoros
Equatorial Guinea
Gambia
Guadeloupe
Guinee Bissau
Iceland
Luxembourg
Macao
Malta
Martinique
Netherlands Antilles
Réunion
Surinam

500 000 - 1 000 000 inhabitants

Bhutan
Botswana
Cyprus
Fiji
Gabon
Guyana
Mauritius
Namibia
Oman
Swaziland
United Arab Emirates

1 000 000 - 2 000 000 inhabitants

Central African Republic
Congo
Jordan
Kuwait
Lesotho
Liberia
Mauritania
Mongolian People's Republic
Panama
Trinidad and Tobago
Ulster
Yemen People's Democratic Republic

III

A MODEL FOR THE MILLENIUM?

In Chapter 6 I briefly indicated how a model of the process space on the mega level, encompassing all economic processes past, present and future, might be set up with the added bonus of a quasi-fixed point, in reference to which economic analysis of distribution could for practical purposes be regarded as cardinal. As this was a side issue, cropping up in the study of very small economies, but possibly too important to be bypassed, it was expedient to write this appendix.

The arguments leading up to the concept of a quasi-cardinal model of human existence on Earth are very simple. They turn on the relationship between human rights and the physical requirements for the livability of human life. Differentials in the livability of human life mirrors differences in economic and social development to such an extent that indicators of livability levels can be used as proxies for levels and stages of under- and overdevelopment.

The latter term can be given an operational meaning by defining full development as the state in which humanly rewarding lives and a full honouring of human rights are materially possible, not for some but for all members of a society. The spending of resources in excess of this livability target constitutes overdevelopment, if not waste in the face of poverty.

The state of full development, as described here, is closely linked to the optimal bundle of human rights. Let me explain this. Present codifications of human rights may be termed immature if not embryonal, but it is not hard to discern the course of their ultimate development towards a stable equilibium of the rights of each individual with the equal rights of every other individual. That equilibrium bundle of human rights is the optimal one, and the level of livability that is required for its full honouring marks the zero position on a quasi-cardinal scale of under- and overdevelopment.

Though present formulations of fundamental rights are strongly biased toward juridical and political (mal-) practices, they are meant also to include the basic right to the bare necessities of life in terms of food, shelter, clothing, education and health care. Such rights, however natural they are, are far from easy to formulate in a juridical sense. An unqualified right to be given these necessities would discriminate between those entitled to receive and those obliged to give. So the right to basic necessities may be implied rather than given in a right to paid work, that would make it possible for people to stand on their own feet and earn their keep, including support of a system of social security caring for their young, old and infirm.

Let us now consider the possible extent of human rights. As even the most ephemeral and spiritual of rights involves the allocation of productive forces to its codification, institution, honouring and safeguarding, the limits of human rights are, in an aggregate sense, the limits of availability of these forces, either directly or condensed in the form of goods and services. If, in first approximation, we take 'income' to stand for the aggregate of material requirements for the effectuation of a particular bundle of human rights, it should be clear that its theoretical lower limit is the point where this income is too low to sustain human life. Human rights not safeguarding the right to live would be a contradiction in terms.

This theoretical lower limit has to be available not to some, but to all, present and future. This claim in its aggregate, against the resources of the essentially closed system of our world is the rock bottom floor of human existence as a natural species. But it is by no means the floor of humanly worthwhile existence. Life at the lowest level that is biologically possible is inhuman. People should be able to live acceptable and awarding lives, that afford the scope for happiness. The aggregated claim resulting from a correspondingly heavier bundle of human rights implies a much higher floor for humanised existence.

There is also a ceiling. Human rights could not possibly include the right to a massive golden crown studded with large diamonds for everybody, because there is not enough to go around. The aggregate human rights claim against resources cannot exceed the total of resources contained in the system. The theoretical ceiling of the human rights package is associated with equal distribution of income and wealth over humanity present and future. Its feasible ceiling is much lower as there are interpersonal and intertemporal inequalities. This is a factual statement, not implying that inequalities are in themselves unethical or at variance with human rights. There is a trade-off between liberty and equality, and the balance between them must be sought between the jungle of unlimited individual liberty and the anthilll of complete equality. Inequality as a concomitant of liberty is a dimension of the livability of human life.

As was already stated above, there exists a point of equilibrium, where the rights of any individual balance with the equal rights of every other individual. The concept of human rights, in its further development, approaches this point asymptotically. The honouring of human rights depends on the necessary but not sufficient condition of availability of the required physical resources. The aggregate of minimally required resources and the total of resources within the system, constitute together an envelope around human life. Let us now turn to the question whether it is feasible to think up a workable model embodying these notions. The next question is how that model might be used in economic analysis and planning.

At first sight an admissible simplification in model building of this kind is to regard the point of convergence of the development of human rights as a fixed point, with an associated fixed point somewhere in the central region of a model of the envelope of resources. Now get this: individual fundamental rights are NOT competing claims on limited resources, but they are the rules of the game, according to which human beings fit in with one another. Changes in rules are not unthinkable, but once a stable balance between individual rights is achieved further changes would upset the balance and not have the common support required for a shift to an other point. The pendulum would swing back.

Associated with the point of equilibrium we may model a vector of livability indicators, marking the requirements in a material sense for the honouring of a fully developed bundle of human rights. The concept of a bounded realm for human existence will be a starting point for first estimations of minimal and maximal values of the separate elements of the vector.

These estimates are not estimates of constants, because the magnitudes are subject to changes. At least within the model we may neglect changes through forces from outside, and direct our attention to ongoing changes caused by endogeneous forces. Depletion of unrenewable resources by some groups or generations will change the bordering conditions of possible future developments. Wars and major natural calamities may have similar negative effects. But technological, organizational and social developments may widen the material scope for the totality of human life. If there are dramatic changes in the range of separate livability indicators this may effect the 'optimal' pro capita values of these indicators that are associated with the human rights equilibrium. So we are definitely on less firm ground when introducing the simplifying assumption that these 'optimal' values of the vector elements are constants, marking the zero positions on partial scales of livability.

For the present, while estimates of these values are lacking, and we have to content ourselves with slowly working our way inward from the outside, this flaw of the model will hardly bother us. But much later, when the model has been improved to the level where the first proper estimates of equilibrium values become feasible, this heroic assumption will cause trouble. We will cross this bridge when we come to it. Much water will pass beneath it before we do.

Once we have made the assumption, we may redefine development as increases of livability levels up to the zero marks, and class movement beyond that level as overdevelopment. Acceptable overdevelopment would be the case where this does not detract from the possibilities of others to attain full development, whereas overdevelopment favouring some groups or generations at the expense of the possibilities of others would in fact be an infringment on human rights.

The outline of our mega-model is at this stage still vague and sketchy. But we may notice that its concepts encompass all kinds of imaginable partial models. Among these are classes of models structurally akin to the mega model, because they describe process spaces and/or potential outcomes spaces of economic processes or clusters of these processes. Those models may be regarded as breakdowns of the mega model. Decomposition of this model and its sub-models is possible, not only spatially and along the time axis, but also according to a host of other classifications that are applicable to human societies and activities. Examples may be models applying to particular regions, to future availability of particular resources, or to particular classes or groups of people. Allowing for fallacies of composition, the complete set of these submodels adds up to the mega model. Any magnitude in the mega model is the aggregate of the corresponding magnitudes of all sub-models. Even fairly rough estimates of the global aggregates can be put to use in reducing the margins of error of the sub-models, as they are broken down further and further down the scale to the smallest unit: the action perimeter of a subject confronted with a problem of choice between alternatives, and the potential outcomes set associated with this act. Scientific progress down the scale from large to smaller systems is the right way for systematic reduction of margins of error and uncertainty.

Compare the direction of this approach with the usual one, which is a direct descendant of the armchair reflections of early economists on the so-called rational behaviour of a fictitious homo economicus, which they had to invent for want of scientific knowledge of human behaviour. Even now such knowledge is far from complete, and, anyway, it is outside the scope of our discipline and economists should not dabble in it. An approach to economics that does not rest on any assumptions as to human conduct is methodologically superior to standing theories still permeated by outdated views on behaviour and rationality. Especially so as many of these theories are induced from theories on smaller systems, increasing the margins of error and uncertainty up the scale.

Let us take another look now at the concept of the livability vector. In model building the nature and number of its elements may be freely chosen to fit the purpose of the analysis. As 'income' livability may be reduced to a one-dimensional magnitude. At the other extreme it may list separately the complete array of goods and services to be found in a fully developed society. In between, the elements may be defined in any way that fits the purpose of the analysis. For instance, at the production factor level we may define a livability vector element representing the yearly pro capita energy use in the total system, to be compared with statistics on pro capita energy use. This would immediately show that in our present world many people have to make shift with much less than any conservative estimate of the human rights equivalent of this magnitude, whereas others are ostentatiously widely overshooting the target. Possible strategies to make the distribution of energy answer the human rights requirements are redistribution and/or an increase of total energy available within the system, to increase the shares of the have-nots without rationing the haves. If these strategies together were found to be inadequate, this would mean that a full complement of human rights could permanently not be brought in reach of all, unless the number of people was reduced to a level where adequate shares could be available to all. The material aspects of human rights are ultimately a matter of life and death. This will be visible also when the attention is turned to any other facet of the livability concept. Livability is the touchstone for human viability.

Yearly energy use per head is also convenient as an example how distribution may be mapped in the mega model and its decompositions. Categories of classification include nation, region, income class, ethnic group etc. For each subsystem the value of the indicator for a given period may be estimated. The set of these estimates constitutes a multidimensional view of the distribution of energy use throughout the system. Time series of these partial indicators may also be constructed. Their analysis is bound to show that they are not mutually independent. This interdependency is a sufficiently strong reason not to limit the analysis of plans to change energy use within a sub-system to the effects on that sub-system only, but to see also what changes are induced in other sub-systems.

This reasoning can be extended to all other aspects of livability. It leads to the desirability of one particular use of the method: to plot and plan the distribution of livability from the global level down to large, less large, and ever smaller sub-systems. Distribution problems would thus in a mutually consistent way be accomodated in one analytical framework, where the interactions of proposed or implemented changes may be made explicit. If mundial agreement is possible on overall policy goals like continuity, equity, peace and welfare, policies for subsystems could be rated for their consistency with the overall targets for the mega-system. Long term planning for humanity as a whole in terms of distribution would emerge as a distinct possibility.

As all economic activities have their distributional consequences, all economic problems could through their distributional transforma-tions be accomodated in the same framework. For instance, econo-mic development causes changes in inputs and outputs in an econo-my, and induces changes in the patterns of distribution within the essentially closed overall system. Long term distributional monito-ring and planning could make the distributional consequences of growth explicit long before they have overtaken us.

Human rights apply not only to present generations, but also to those unborn. Mundial planning of distribution should safeguard their interests as well. To do this by discounting methods is arbitrary, as the discount rate is optional. Moreover, the reduction of future magnitudes to present values tends to turn planners into myopics. It is much better to plan for the Millenium.

What I mean by this is a model with a time horizon of one thousand years, that is updated every ten or twenty years. If and when threats to the system or its aims appear within this planning period there will be, in the ideal case, almost a thousand years either to solve the problem or to prepare in the best possible way for the end, if that is unavoidable.

This ideal situation is not what we will find if in the near future we manage to set up a first makeshift version of the Millenial model. If it is any good it will show threats to our continued existence not vaguely and distant, near the time horizon, but right under our noses in the next if not in this century. Even so the model may help us to plot a course to safer waters. Once the model has been set up, its analytical and predictive value will increase steadily with use, through feedback information. That is, if we manage to solve our major problems in time. In that case we will have descendants, less likely to get themselves in a similar fix. That is, if we manage to leave them the tools for long term prediction and planning. To assist in the founding of a Millenium that may last thousands of years is a worth while aim for all economists.